The Dreamer's Almanac

The Dreamer's Almanac

Understanding the Messages from Your Subconscious

Sasha Parker

THUNDER BAY
P·R·E·S·S

San Diego, California

THUNDER BAY
P · R · E · S · S

Thunder Bay Press
An imprint of Baker & Taylor Publishing Group
10350 Barnes Canyon Road
San Diego, CA 92121
www.thunderbaybooks.com

All notations of errors or omissions should be addressed to Thunder Bay Press,
Editorial Department, at the above address. All other correspondence (author
inquiries, permissions) concerning the content of this book should be
addressed to Saraband, Suite 202, 98 Woodlands Road, Glasgow G6 6HB, UK

ISBN-13: 978-1-60710-079-9
ISBN-10: 1-60710-079-7

Library of Congress Cataloging-in-Publication Data available upon request

Printed in China

1 2 3 4 5 13 12 11 10 09

This book is dedicated to Clare Gibson, my mentor as a dream interpreter
and supervisor of my research into the world of dreams and their meanings.
The interpretations here are inspired by her work, and in particular,
her book *The Secret Life of Dreams.*

CONTENTS

INTRODUCTION

"In the following pages, I shall demonstrate that there is a psychological technique which makes it possible to interpret dreams, and that on the application of this technique, every dream will reveal itself as a psychological structure, full of significance, and one which may be assigned to a specific place in the psychic activities of the waking state."

—Sigmund Freud
The Interpretation of Dreams (1900)

Since the appearance in 1900 of Sigmund Freud's radical and hugely influential work *Die Traumdeutung (The Interpretation of Dreams)*, the man who became known as the "father of psychology" has been considered by some the "father," too, of dream interpretation. But the idea that our dreams cast light on our minds, our thoughts, and emotions, or tell us anything meaningful about ourselves, is far from a modern one. Dreams have intrigued humankind since the earliest times, and explanations have been sought as to their meanings.

DREAMS AND RELIGION

References to dreams, and clues to their hold on the human imagination, are found in many examples of ancient literature and art. It is thought that the Babylonian poem the *Epic of Gilgamesh* (dating from around 1760 BC) contains the oldest documented treatment of dreams, but the dreams that are described in the Judeo–Christian scriptures are perhaps the best known of early writings on the subject, and they have therefore had a greater influence on the history of our understanding of our nighttime cerebral adventures. There are around 700 references to dreams in the bible.

Many of these biblical dreams have been seen by those of the Judeo-Christian tradition as straightforward revelations from God. In Genesis 28:10–17, for example, it is told that Jacob was dreaming of angels ascending and descending a

ladder reaching up to heaven when the Lord appeared by his side and promised him and his descendants the land on which he was lying. Some biblical dreams provide religious or moral instruction, however, as is made clear in Job 33:15–16: "In dreams, in visions of the night, when deepest sleep falls upon men, while they sleep on their beds, God makes them listen, and his correction strikes them with terror."

8

Page 6: *Our dreaming imaginations are as limitless as the stars of the night sky.*
Opposite: *Jacob dreamed of a ladder reaching up to heaven, flanked by angels, and interpreted it as a message from God, as told in the Book of Genesis.*
Right: *Nebuchadnezzar, the biblical king, was mystified by his dream of a tree. Dream trees may refer to the Tree of Life, and individual species or types of tree have their own, specific meanings.*

Some of the dreams recorded in the Old Testament puzzled the dreamers, notably King Nebuchadnezzar, for whom the meaning of his dream of a tree confounded him, as well as his "magicians, exorcists, Chaldeans, and diviners," until Daniel explained that the tree symbolized the king himself (Daniel 4). Many psychologists today would reach a similar conclusion, and would also agree with Joseph's explanation that in his dream of the sun, moon, and eleven stars (Genesis 37:9–11), the sun represented his father, the moon, his mother, and the stars, his eleven brothers. Joseph became known for the ability to interpret not only his own dreams, but those of others, a talent that was responsible for his release from prison on the orders of the Pharaoh.

There are numerous examples of biblical dreams that were interpreted as precognitive, as messages from God, or as having other meanings. Some of the most important of these

Above: *Perhaps the most famous of biblical dreamers, Joseph was taken from his jail cell into the service of the Pharaoh (probably Amenemhat III) because of his dream-interpretation skills.*
Right: *Daniel interpreted dreams for Nebuchadnezzar, among others, but his faith led him to be cast into a den of lions—a fate he survived, miraculously.*

10

Left: *This second- or third-century sculpture from the ancient kingdom of Gandhara (part of present-day Pakistan and Afghanistan) illustrates Queen Maya's dream of how the Buddha, her son, would be conceived.*

can be found in Genesis 20:3–8 (Abimelech's dream); Genesis 40:8–19 (Pharaoh's butler and baker's dream); Genesis 41:1–36 (Pharaoh's own dream); Daniel 2:1–45 (another of Nebuchadnezzar's dreams); Judges 7:13–14 (a soldier's dream, interpreted by Gideon); and several in the Book of Matthew, including Matthew 1:20–24 (Joseph's dream) and Matthew 27:19 (the dream of Pilate's wife, concerning the persecution of Jesus).

Most other major religions, including Hinduism and Islam, similarly credit dreams with similar revelatory or predictive qualities: according to Buddhist lore, for instance, Queen Maya became aware that she had conceived a son (the future Buddha) when she dreamed of a white elephant descending into her womb.

ANCIENT AND INDIGENOUS CULTURES

Such was the importance attached to dreams and their significance in ancient Greece and Rome that dream interpreters were sometimes engaged to accompany and advise military generals, in the belief that dreams contained guidance from the gods. Like the dreams related in the Judeo-Christian bible and in other religious texts, which were described as divine messages that were intended to inform, reveal, predict, warn, or chastise, they were seen by ancient Egyptians, Greeks, and Romans as having these functions. In addition, the ancients believed that dreams had healing powers, and therefore tried to incubate, or consciously induce, curative dreams at sanctuaries that were attached to the temples of their gods of medicine. These included

Left: *Asclepius, the ancient Greek god associated with dream healing.*
Right: *Hippocrates (c. 460–370 BC), trained as a physician at an asclepieion (or healing temple) on the isle of Kos.*
Opposite: *In ancient Greece, dream interpreters were considered important enough that they sometimes accompanied generals in battle. Shown here is the Battle of Issus, 333 BC, fought between Alexander the Great and Darius III of Persia, in a painting by Albrecht Altdorfer.*

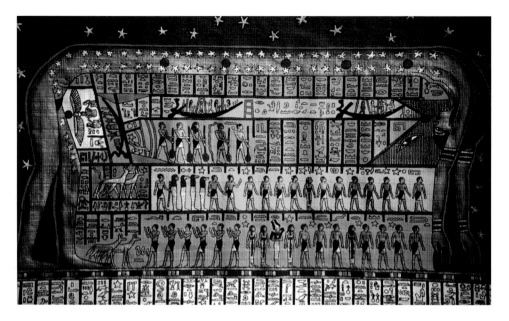

Imhotep and Serapis in Egypt, Asclepius in Greece, and his counterpart Aesculapius in Rome. They hoped to invoke divine assistance, and the resulting dreams were interpreted by dream specialists. Evidence of the importance of dreams in ancient Egypt is seen in the hieroglyphics that have survived on papyruses around four thousand years old.

In common with the ancient Babylonians, the Egyptians, Greeks, and Romans made a distinction between positive dreams, which they believed emanated from benevolent gods—that is, as long as they were properly propitiated—and nightmares, which were thought to be omens inflicted on sleepers by malevolent demons. The Babylonians paid the priests of Mamu to intercede with their goddess of dreams to prevent such dreams from coming true.

In China, it was believed that the soul left the body during sleep, and dreams were the activities of the soul that took place in another realm. It was considered dangerous to waken someone suddenly, because the soul could be elsewhere at the time, and unable to return to the body.

It could be said that for as long as people have been dreaming, dreams have been accorded supernatural significance by most of the world's spiritual traditions, but there are certain cultures to which the phenomenon of dreaming is fundamental, both to their sense of identity and to the regulation of their society.

Opposite: *Uluru, the iconic rock formation in Australia's Northern Territory, had a central place in the spiritual life of the indigenous people, for whom the Dreaming was the time when the earth and its creatures were created.*
Right: *This illustration from a bronze plaque originated in Benin, in western Africa. It shows men guarding the house of their tribal council, at which dreams were recounted and interpreted.*

In Australia, the Aborigines believe that the landscape itself, along with the creatures and plants that inhabit it, was created by their supernatural ancestors (some of which were human, others animals, and yet others hybrid creatures) upon waking from their slumber during the "Dreaming," or the "Dreamtime" (*altjiranga* or *alcheringa*). Not only did these ancestors lay down the rules and rituals by which Aboriginal life should be lived, but it is also said that they established a mystical connection between their descendants and their totem animals and plants before returning to their sleeping state.

Many African and Native American tribes cherish remarkably similar totemic creation myths, and, what's more, often believe that dreams provide a direct conduit to their ancestors' wisdom. Dream-pooling plays a crucial role in such societies, when tribal members may gather together for the specific purpose of collectively incubating a dream focusing on a tribal issue, then listen to each other recount the dreams that they have had, ponder possible interpretations, and if any dream seems particularly important, or a pattern of dreams can be discerned, tailor tribal policy to the dreamland message. Like many modern dream interpreters, other Native American tribes believe that dreams express our deepest, and most hidden, desires. Another view of dreaming that is shared by some modern-day dream researchers is held by the Inuit of Hudson Bay, among other people, who are convinced that the soul leaves the body and goes wandering while the dreamer is sleeping.

EARLY DREAM INTERPRETERS

The ancient Egyptians are thought to be the oldest culture to develop a regularized system of dream interpretation. They believed in a form of the contrary-dream theory, which holds that a positive dream heralds a downturn in waking fortunes, while a nightmare foretells an improvement in the dreamer's real-life circumstances. It seems, however, that it was the ancient Greeks who first delved deeper into the possible reasons why humans dream, in doing so proposing a variety of theories suggesting that dreams are internal communications rather than messages from an external source.

Most of these dream theorists, as far as we know today, were philosophers, the earliest being Heraclitus (*c.* 544–483 BC), who observed, "The waking have one world in common; sleepers have each a private world of their own." In commenting that "The virtuous man is content to *dream* what a wicked

"We must, in the next place, investigate the subject of the dream, and first inquire to which of the faculties of the soul it presents itself, i.e. whether the affection is one which pertains to the faculty of intelligence or to that of sense-perception; for these are the only faculties within us by which we acquire knowledge. If, then, the exercise of the faculty of sight is actual seeing, that of the auditory faculty, hearing, and, in general that of the faculty of sense-perception, perceiving; and if there are some perceptions common to the senses, such as figure, magnitude, motion, &c., while there are others, as color, sound, taste, peculiar [each to its own sense]; and further, if all creatures, when the eyes are closed in sleep, are unable to see, and the analogous statement is true of the other senses, so that manifestly we perceive nothing when asleep; we may conclude that it is not by sense-perception we perceive a dream."

— Aristotle

Right: *Aristotle (384–322 BC) wrote extensively on the subject of dream interpretation. He rejected the notion that dreams were messages from the gods, proposing instead an early form of modern-day psychological theories.*

man really *does*," Plato (*c.* 427–347 BC) may have anticipated Freud in proposing a wish-fulfillment explanation for dreams. His pupil Aristotle (384–322 B.C.) proposed a simple form of Jung's theory of the collective unconscious by speculating that, because people's dreams have similar themes, they may arise from a shared

Above: *Some claim that the man seated at center left, pen in hand, in Raphael's* School of Athens *(1510–11), is the influential dream researcher Artemidorus, although his identity is not known for certain.*

source. Aristotle also emphatically rejected the prevalent classical idea that dreams were divine oracles, stating in his work *De Divinatione Per Somnum (On Divination Through Sleep)* that "most so-called prophetic dreams are to be classed as mere coincidences..."

The "father of medicine," the Greek physician Hippocrates (*c.* 460–377 BC), first advanced the view that some dream-world symbols reflect the condition of the dreamer's body (a deluge of water denoting an excess of blood, for instance), and should therefore be regarded as diagnostic tools. Perhaps the most influential dream theorist of this age was a Roman, however, namely Artemidorus (AD 138–180), the author of *Oneirocriticon (The Interpretation of Dreams)* and the first dedicated dream researcher to focus on both symbolism and common types of dreams. Artemidorus's broad conclusion was that, while dreamland symbols can have general meanings, their personal significance to the dreamer has to be taken into account when interpreting dreams, along with the dreamer's personality and individual circumstances.

Although the early Christian Church fathers respected dreams as the bearers of potentially illuminating spiritual insights, the advent of the Middle Ages and the increasingly repressive control of the Roman Catholic Church (which regarded dreams as the devil's work) over Western society put a halt to any serious attempt to study dreams. With the waning of the restrictive influence of the Church during the eighteenth century, however, members of the German Romantic Movement turned their attention to their dreams in a quest to explore the free expression of human feeling and individuality, in doing so identifying the unconscious as the source of their dreams. Thereafter, there was a general revival of interest in the meaning of dreams during the nineteenth century, mainly as a result of the publication of countless popular dream dictionaries like Raphael's *Royal Book of Dreams* of 1830 (by the English astrologer Robert Cross Smith), although such publications were essentially frivolous guides characterized by their fortune-telling flavor.

ON SLEEPING

Before turning to modern dream interpretation, an understanding of the functions of sleep is helpful. Sleep is so crucial to our health and well-being that we spend something like a third of our lives sleeping. When we consciously relinquish control of our bodies and abandon ourselves to sleep, the unconscious mind comes to the fore, giving rise to dreams. Although the purpose of neither sleep nor dreams is yet fully understood, the pioneering work that Nathaniel Kleitman, Eugene Aserinsky, and William Dement carried out at the University of Chicago's Department of Physiology's sleep laboratory during the 1950s provided the first scientific breakthrough into understanding what

Above: *Sleep is vital to our health and well-being, and it is likely that dreaming is just as crucial to our psychological well-being.*

happens while we are sleeping. This was an important foundation that subsequent researchers have built upon in giving us an increasingly clear picture of the nocturnal activities of the mind.

Once you have drifted off to sleep, your body and brain undergo radical changes that make them markedly different from their waking state. When you begin to doze, researchers believe that you rapidly progress through four stages of slow-wave sleep that form the basis of a cycle that repeats itself four or five times over an eight-hour period of sleep.

At first, both your body and brain become increasingly relaxed, your heartbeat slows, as does your breathing, and your eyes start to roll from side to side. During this first stage, you are neither fully conscious nor completely unconscious and could quickly become wide awake again if disturbed. At this point of light sleep, you are in the hypnagogic state (and shortly before waking up you are in a similar condition, called the hypnapompic state), when you may experience muscular spasms; hallucinations and distorted images may float before your closed eyes; and you may hear voices.

In the second stage, your eyes continue to roll, your breathing and heart rate become ever slower, your blood pressure drops, your brain activity decreases, and you are increasingly oblivious to the noises of the outside world (although you could still be woken relatively easily).

Having entered the third stage of sleep, you are now sleeping soundly. Your heart rate drops further, as does your breathing rate and body temperature.

Next, you enter a type of deep slumber known as non-rapid-eye-movement (N.R.E.M.) sleep, when your brain is operating at its slowest. Your brain is now able to take stock of your body and releases a growth hormone to repair damaged tissues and stimulate growth. It is also thought that your brain's hippocampus records memories of the events of the day during this stage of sleep. It would now be quite difficult to wake you, and although you may suffer an attack of the night terrors, get up and sleep-walk, or dream nebulous, thought-based dreams, you will rarely be able to recall any such nocturnal experiences. If you awaken suddenly at this stage, you will believe that you did not dream at all.

This slow-wave sleep cycle lasts for about ninety minutes, and at the end of stage four you move back through the cycle again, through stages three and two, to one, at which point you enter a phase named rapid-eye-movement (R.E.M.) sleep. Now your brain waves speed up, your heartbeat and breathing become faster and more irregular, your blood pressure rises, and your eyes dart rapidly around behind your eyelids (which is why R.E.M. sleep is so named), although your body is otherwise in a state of paralysis. Most of the dreams that we remember occur during R.E.M. sleep, when the brain's cortex is highly active. After around ten minutes of R.E.M. sleep, you enter stages two, three, and four again, and continue to move backward and forward through the sleep cycle during the course of the night. As the cycle progresses, each R.E.M. phase becomes longer, with the last—around thirty to forty-five minutes long—containing your longest, most visual, vivid, and active dreams. Of all of your dreams, these are the ones that you are most likely to recall on waking.

While N.R.E.M. sleep is vital for physical rest, repair, and recuperation, dream-packed R.E.M. sleep is crucial to our psychological well-being. Why, then, do we dream? Numerous theories have been put forward in explanation, but a conclusive, scientifically proven answer remains elusive. Among functions like sifting through events and sorting memories, helping to prevent the brain from becoming burdened with an overload of unimportant information, it is widely believed today that dreaming fulfills a profound emotional human need.

FREUD, JUNG, AND MODERN DREAM INTERPRETATION

When he wrote *The Interpretation of Dreams* at the turn of the twentieth century, the Austrian psychoanalyst Sigmund Freud (1856–1939) shocked the Western world to the core, the reverberations of its impact spreading rapidly after its publication in 1900. The reason for the outrage that greeted his book in a relatively prudish age was its conclusion that our dreams are wish-fulfillment fantasies that have their origins in our infantile urges, especially our sexual desires.

Freud believed that the human mind has three components: the id, the primitive, unconscious mind; the ego, the conscious mind, which regulates or represses the id's instincts with a kind of self-protective defense mechanism because it considers them disturbingly contrary to social norms; and the superego, the conscience that, in turn, modifies the ego. The id, he stated, is governed by the pleasure principle (which

Above: *Sigmund Freud, the Austrian psychoanalyst who shocked the world with his theories of the meanings of our dreams.*

seeks to gratify unconscious needs), and the instincts that the ego represses, to help us fit in with the wider world, are the sexual drives that we first experience as early as in our infancy.

While we are dreaming, Freud believed, the id is in the ascendant: it expresses the urges that the ego (which relaxes its censorship while we are sleeping) represses when we are conscious. These urges are expressed as symbols, because if the underlying wishes were portrayed literally, they would be understood by the ego, which would immediately be shocked into wakefulness, when it would again repress them. If a dream is to be successfully interpreted, its manifest content (that is, the symbols that the dreamer recalls appearing in the dream on waking) must be stripped of its various dis-

guises to reveal its latent content, or the drives that the symbols represent. The way that Freud advocated achieving this goal was by using free association, or spontaneously voicing the responses that immediately spring to mind when certain key words relating to the dream are pronounced, thereby trying to elude the censorship of the ego at the same time as tapping into the id's thought processes. This free association,

Above: Freud (left) and Jung (front, center) in Massachusetts with other academics in the emerging science of psychology.
Opposite: Just as hypnosis is believed to be a vehicle for discovering the secrets of the unconscious mind, so dreams may reveal them, whether directly or in symbolic language.

Freud believed, could give an enlightening insight into the nature of the dreamer's unconscious instincts.

The Swiss analytical psychologist Carl Gustav Jung (1875–1961) was originally an enthusiastic supporter of Freud's ideas, and the two men collaborated closely for a number of years. But Jung's increasing disagreement with Freud's theories caused their relationship to end shortly before World War I. In his posthumously published book

Memories, Dreams, Reflections (1962), he wrote: "I was never able to agree with Freud that the dream is a 'façade' behind which its meaning lies hidden—a meaning already known, but maliciously, so to speak, withheld from consciousness. To me dreams are a part of nature, which harbors no intention to deceive, but expresses something as best it can, just as a plant grows or an animal seeks food as best it can." As well as his rejection of the Freudian "dream-as-a-façade" viewpoint, Jung felt that there was far more behind dreams than simply the expression of sexual desires. He also postulated that the contents of the unconscious mind were not merely determined by personal experience, but were shared with all other humans. He subsequently evolved his theory

"THE UTTERANCE OF THE UNCONSCIOUS"

The view that dreams are merely imaginary fulfillments of suppressed wishes has long since been superseded. It is certainly true that there are dreams which embody suppressed wishes and fears, but what is there which the dream cannot on occasion embody? Dreams may give expression to ineluctable truths, to philosophical pronouncements, illusions, wild fantasies, memories, plans, anticipations, irrational experiences, even telepathic visions, and heaven knows what besides. One thing we ought never to forget: almost the half of our lives is passed in a more or less unconscious state. The dream is specifically the utterance of the unconscious. We may call consciousness the daylight realm of the human psyche, and contrast it with the nocturnal realm of unconscious psychic activity which we apprehend as dreamlike fantasy. It is certain that consciousness consists not only of wishes and fears, but of vastly more than these, and it is highly probable that the unconscious psyche contains a wealth of contents and living forms equal to or even greater than does consciousness, which is characterized by concentration, limitation and exclusion.

—Carl Jung
"Dream-Analysis,"
Modern Man in Search of a Soul (1933)

of the collective unconscious, which he described as a kind of storehouse of inherited patterns of experiences, instincts, and memories common to humankind that are expressed in dreams in the form of universal images or symbols. He called these symbols archetypes.

According to Jung, we have inherited our collective unconscious and its archetypes from our instinct-influenced primeval ancestors, and "their origin can only be explained by assuming them to be deposits of the constantly repeated experiences of humanity" (*On the Psychology of the Unconscious*, 1917). And because, Jungian theory states, the psyche consists of the personal unconscious and the collective unconscious (with the conscious mind making up the trio of psychic components), when we encounter a mystifying symbol in dreamland, it is crucial to decide whether it relates to our personal experience or is instead an archetype. Many archetypes are familiar to

Above and left: *Archetypal figures, like the prince above and the trickster, left, appear in fairy tales the world over.*

us through our knowledge of religious symbolism, myths, legends, and fairy tales. This is why Jung proposed that it is the dreamer, who knows him- or herself better than anyone else can, who is best equipped to interpret his or her dreams, but by direct, not free, association because, as Jung put it, "Free association will bring out all of my complexes, but hardly ever the meaning of a dream. To understand the dream's meaning, I must stick as close as possible to the dream images." (*The Practical Use of Dream-analysis*, 1931). By this, Jung meant concentrating on the symbol alone as you list all of the qualities with which you associate it.

But why does the unconscious mind screen archetypal symbols on the dream screen? Jung believed that it is for purposes of psychic self-regulation by the self (our core, or essential, identity), in order to promote healthy development and eventually bring the conscious and unconscious minds into a state of perfect equilibrium or psychic wholeness, which he called individuation. Because the unconscious (be it personal or collective) can only express itself fully in dreams, it autonomously

Left and Opposite: In order to understand and benefit from the unconscious mind's messages in our dreams, Jung believed, we must learn to decode the symbolic language that dreams contain.

strives to compensate for the influence that the conscious mind wields over us when we are awake by conveying symbolic dreamland messages that reflect our current progress in life. These messages bring repressed or neglected urges to the fore, offer guidance, or warn us that we are straying from the path, or destiny, that would ultimately lead to fulfillment. But, as Jung explained, before we can benefit from the intuitive wisdom of the personal or collective unconscious, we must consciously strive to understand its symbolic language and become familiar with its visual vocabulary.

While the revolutionary theories of Freud and Jung have become seminal to dream interpretation, the work of later psychologists has furthered our understanding of dreams, as well as proposing alternative methods of decoding them.

As the originator of the inferiority-complex theory, it is perhaps not surprising that the Austrian "individual psychologist" Alfred Adler (1870–1937) believed that dreams are on the one hand concerned with wish fulfillment because they enable the individual dreamer to attain the superiority, or power, in the dream world that is denied to him or her in waking life, and, on the other, with problem solving. As far as Adler was concerned, "The purpose of dreams must be in the feelings they arouse." He went on to say in *What Life Should Mean to You* (reprinted in 1962), "We must arrive at the conclusion that dreams are an

Left and Opposite: According to Alfred Adler (left), we can compensate for our difficulties in the waking world by having pleasant dreams (opposite).

attempt to make a bridge between an individual's style of life and his present problems without making new demands of the style of life. The style of life is the master of dreams. It will always arouse the feelings that the individual needs."

Fritz Perls (1893–1970), the noted Gestalt psychologist, devised an often effective method of making sense of a baffling dream, namely by adopting a noninterpretive interviewing technique. Perls, who believed that dreams project hidden aspects of our personalities, advocated placing two chairs opposite each other, one earmarked for you and the other for the dream. While sitting in "your" chair, he suggested that you address the "dream's" chair and ask a character or object that featured in the dream what it was trying to say. Then you should swap chairs and try to adopt the dream's "mindset" before answering your question, moving to and fro between the two chairs in this way until your answers have clarified the meaning of your dream.

The American dream specialist Gayle Delaney also advised using an interviewing technique, but in this case addressing the questions directly to yourself (or else asking someone else to quiz you). The queries in Delaney's list include the following. How did the dream make you feel? What was the dream setting, and can you connect it with your waking life? Who were the people in your dream, and what are they like in the waking world? Were there any objects in your dream, and, if so, can you describe them? How do each of these aspects of your dream relate to your waking life? What occurred in the dream, and does it remind you of anything that has happened in real life?

The interpretive hints given in this book are a fusion of all of these groundbreaking theories and techniques, but especially those of Jung and Freud.

CLASSIFYING DREAMS

Clearly, every dream is individual, even if it resembles another in content. Aside from the events and symbols within dreams, not all dreams are similar in origin, cause, or function, either. There are a number of common categories, or types, of dreams. Each of us is likely to experience some, though not all, of the most common types.

LITERAL DREAMS Literal, factual, or processing dreams are replays of your recent experiences in the waking world. Although they usually have little symbolic significance, by reviewing the day's occurrences they may sometimes throw light on a previously unrecognized aspect of the dreamer's situation. External stimuli, such as the tone of a ringing telephone, can also be incorporated into literal dreams.

HOWE'S SEWING MACHINE.

PHYSIOLOGICAL DREAMS Physiological, or body, dreams reflect the actual state of the dreamer's body, so if, for example, you became dehydrated during the night, you may have had a physiological dream in which you were parched with thirst. Such dreams may sometimes highlight the onset or progress of a more serious physical condition, when they are usually recurrent.

Above: *A crucial detail of the sewing machine illustrated above came about as a result of a problem-solving dream by its inventor, Elias Howe.*

PROBLEM-SOLVING DREAMS If you went to sleep thinking about a problem, you may have found that you woke with the solution running through your brain. This probably happened because you had already unconsciously solved your problem, and sleeping on it gave your unconscious the opportunity to reveal the answer that had eluded your conscious mind, perhaps in the form of a problem-solving dream. There are some well-known examples of inventions that originated in dreamland after their inventors had consciously failed to make a crucial breakthrough, including the chain-stitch sewing machine that the American inventor Elias Howe (1819–67) patented in 1846, which was prompted by his dream of Africans carrying spears with eye-shaped holes in their flattened tips, which his waking mind translated into sewing-machine needles. James Watt (1736–1819), the Scottish engineer and inventor of the steam engine, dreamed of molten metal falling from the sky and shaping itself into balls, which gave him the idea for drop-cooling and hence ball bearings. Other famous problem-solving dreams include that of the German chemist August Kekulé von Stradonitz (1829–96), who, while in the hypnagogic state, dreamed of a snake swallowing its tail, resulting in a "eureka!" moment when he realized that the ring theory explains the molecular structure of benzene.

Opposite: The visionary English artist William Blake said that he used his dreams to inspire his extraordinary artwork. ***Below:*** James Watt, who famously had a problem-solving dream.

INSPIRATIONAL DREAMS Many great works of art, music, and literature have stemmed from inspirational dreams, when the unconscious makes us a gift of a creative idea. The mystical work of the English poet and artist William Blake (1757–1827) was reportedly inspired by his dreams, for example, as

And One stood forth from the Divine Family & said

I feel my Spectre rising upon me! Albion! arouze thyself!
Why dost thou thunder with frozen Spectrous wrath against us?
The Spectre is in Giant Man: insane and most deformd
Thou wilt certainly provoke my Spectre against thine in fury!
He has a Sepulcher hewn out of a Rock ready for thee:
And a Death of Eight thousand years forgd by thyself upon
The point of his Spear! if thou persistest to forbid with Laws
Our Emanations, and to attack our secret supreme delights

So Los spoke: But when he saw blue death in Albions feet,
Again he joind the Divine Body, following merciful:
While Albion fled more indignant: revengeful covering

were the paintings of many Surrealist artists, the books of such authors as Robert Louis Stevenson (1850–94), and the compositions of musicians like Guiseppe Tartini (1692–1770).

CATHARTIC AND SAFETY-VALVE DREAMS By immersing us in a dream that evokes a strong emotional reaction, the unconscious gives us the opportunity to express—and relieve—some of the pent-up feelings that we may feel unable to vent in the waking world. These are known as cathartic dreams. If you had a dream in which you lashed out at someone physically, you may have had a safety-valve dream. According to Freud, the unconscious makes us a present of these dreams when we need to let off steam by forcibly expressing pent-up emotions or desires, but are unable to do so in the real world due to a perceived need to behave in accordance with convention.

CONTRARY OR COMPENSATORY DREAMS In a contrary or compensatory dream, the unconscious mind depicts the dreaming self in a completely different situation to that within which we find ourselves during the day. If your waking hours are filled with feelings of grief following the death of a loved one, for example, your dream may compensate for your mourning and depression by immersing you in a light-hearted, happy atmosphere—possibly in the form of your being with your loved one in your dream. Your unconscious may alternatively give you a personality transplant, so that if you are shy, you may revel in the novelty of being superconfident in dreamland. Such dreams are believed to compensate for, or balance, a waking life or personality that has become distinctly skewed in one direction, and may also be advocating incorporating the lifestyle or personal characteristic that your dream highlighted into your waking life.

LUCID DREAMS While you are sleeping, you may sometimes become aware that you are dreaming. Your conscious realization may have been triggered during R.E.M. sleep, either because something about your dream struck you as being incredible or because the mounting fear

Right: *This illustration appears to depict a "false awakening," in which the dreamer thinks that she has just awoken to the sight of a ghost in her bedroom —a frightening, but not uncommon, experience for children.*

that you experienced during a nightmare reached an intolerable peak. It takes time and practice to avoid waking up, but it is possible to train yourself to become a lucid dreamer, when, armed with the rational powers of your conscious mind, you may be able to face the "monsters" that give you nightmares and expose them as being nothing more dangerous than your own fears. You may also be able to control the course of your dreamland experiences to a certain extent, perhaps in order to enjoy wish-fulfillment dreams.

FALSE AWAKENINGS You may have experienced a false awakening during the night if you awoke in the morning convinced that the events that were played out in your dream really happened because your memory of them is so powerful. Researchers believe that many reported sightings of ghosts are due to false awakenings, which happen when you are actually still asleep, but believe, in your slumbering state, that you are awake.

Above: Incubated dreams are the result of focused concentration.
Opposite: Nightmare!

INCUBATED DREAMS

Incubated dreams sometimes occur when you have set your conscious mind on experiencing a particular dream — perhaps to help you to solve a waking problem — the theory being that your unconscious then responds to your conscious suggestion after you have fallen asleep. It is believed that you can encourage such dreams by meditating on your chosen subject or problem, or, if you are hoping to dream of a person, by studying his or her photograph; by visualizing the dream; or by repeating a short sentence describing the nature of the dream that you want to have, or by asking for the answer to your problem, immediately before going to sleep.

MUTUAL DREAMS Although they are rare, mutual dreams occur when two people dream the same dream, sometimes even meeting up in dreamland. Such shared dreams may either arise spontaneously or can be incubated. If you have agreed to share a dream with someone you know (and the best results are achieved by people who are emotionally or physically close), you should decide on the dreamland location together and should both then visualize that setting before going to sleep.

INTRODUCTION

NIGHTMARES AND NIGHT TERRORS

Nightmares are dreams that distress or terrify us, and usually arise when we are feeling anxious or helpless through being exposed to a stressful situation or hostile person in the waking world. Such deeply unpleasant dreams, which occur during R.E.M. sleep, are often recurring, but once we have consciously identified the nightmares' trigger and have then rationally confronted and worked through the unresolved fears and anxieties that it arouses in us, they will usually eventually cease. Night

terrors are related to nightmares, but because they strike during stage four of slow-wave sleep, we rarely remember what happened in the dream, although we are nevertheless left with an overwhelming sense of dread.

OUT-OF-BODY EXPERIENCES

Many researchers dismiss the notion that the mind, consciousness, soul, or spirit has the ability to leave its body and travel through space, yet such experiences have been well documented, even if they are not understood. Also known as astral travel or projection, out-of-body experiences (O.B.E.s) are believed to occur during sleep, as well as at times of physical or emotional trauma (and especially during near-death experiences, or N.D.E.s).

PRECOGNITIVE DREAMS Did Abraham Lincoln (1809–65), the sixteenth president of the United States, really foresee his death a few days before his assassination, when he dreamed of being told that the president had died? Although they are the subject of heated controversy (and most dream researchers dismiss them as either coincidences or the expression of unconscious knowledge), true precognitive, prophetic, or clairvoyant dreams anticipate real-life events that the dreamer has no way of predicting (even unconsciously). It seems that such dreams are more prevalent among people with highly developed psychic abilities, but are nevertheless extremely rare. If you believe that you have had a dream of this nature, make sure that you record and date it so that you have proof of your dream should it really come true.

PAST-LIFE DREAMS If your dream was set in a historical setting, some analysts would say that you relived an actual past-life experience or a previous incarnation, or else assumed the identity of one of your ancestors. Most professional analysts dispute the existence of past-life, or far-memory, and genetic dreams, however.

RECURRING DREAMS Recurring dreams typically plague dreamers when they are consciously worried about an ongoing waking situation, when they are suffering from a phobia, or when they have repressed, rather than resolved, the memory of a traumatic event. When the trigger state of affairs comes to an end in the waking world, so, usually, do the dreams. If, however, they stem from an underlying phobia or trauma, it is thought that the purpose of the unconscious in continuing to expose a dreamer to the cause of his or her horror is to force him or her to haul the memory to the forefront of the conscious mind, to consider it rationally, and to try to come to terms with it. After this, the dream should gradually become less frequent before, it is hoped, finally disappearing. If you suffer from recurring dreams, remember that your unconscious is trying to help, not torment, you, and that it will continue to try to drum home its message until you con-

Above: *Recurring dreams are usually caused by anxiety or phobias.*

sciously receive it, acknowledge it, deal with the problem that prompted it, and thus release yourself from its grip.

TELEPATHIC DREAMS In a typical telepathic dream, someone known to the dreamer appears in dreamland accompanied by a powerful sense of distress, after which the dreamer later learns that that person experienced a real-life crisis (such as the sudden onset of an illness, an accident, or even death) at the precise time that he or she had the dream. It is thought that telepathic transference, or meetings of minds—when the dreamer receives a powerful emotional message signaled by the transmitter, who may not have been aware of communicating in this way—occur between people who have a close emotional connection.

WISH-FULFILLMENT DREAMS By fulfilling our fantasies in dreamland—whether we long to be millionaires, to be admired by others, to be irresistibly desirable, or just to go on vacation—the unconscious is compensating us for an unsatisfying waking existence.

DECODING YOUR DREAMS

Our dream scenarios may seem bizarre when we look back at them from a waking perspective, but most dream analysts believe that our dreams are transmitting messages from our unconscious to our conscious minds, inner communications that have the potential to set us on a richer, and more fulfilling, path in waking life. If we are to reap the riches of our own unconscious minds, however, we must first learn to understand the secret life of dreams. The chapters of this book cover a broad spectrum of dream themes, from those that arouse strong emotional responses like happiness and excitement, anxiety, or anger, to those that puzzle you by focusing on something as mundane as an everyday object—or even something entirely abstract, such as a color or shape. Try to get into the habit of recording your dreams in a diary as soon asyou wake up, because you will forget the details rapidly during the course of the day.

When attempting to interpret your dream, look up the scenario, symbol, or emotion that dominated it. This may involve referring to more than one theme, as well as thinking laterally,

Above: *To understand what your dreams say about your unconscious mind, get into the habit of recording them accurately as soon as you wake up, when the details are fresh in your mind.*

bearing in mind puns and symbols that are pointed to in these pages and in the related themes shown at the top of each page. If these primary meanings do not explain your dream, refer to the index and continue to think of what the dream could have meant to you. Some dreams are interpreted more readily than others, but with time and practice, you will become adept at decoding the messages your unconscious mind serves up night after night.

SELF & OTHERS

Our dreams almost always involve a cast of characters, whether the dreams revolve around our own thoughts and feelings, or center on encounters with family members, friends, or strangers. Sometimes the people in our dreams represent archetypes (a mother figure, perhaps, or our shadow), or perhaps they are aspects of our own personality, acting out a situation that has a parallel in our waking life. This chapter will help you to shed light on the significance of the people in your dreams and whether they are trying to convey an important message, help you to resolve an old emotional wound, or highlight your hopes or fears.

SELF & OTHERS

THE LIFE CYCLE

Related themes:
Pregnancy
Childbirth
New beginnings

BIRTHS

When the unconscious mind calls up the theme of birth into our dreams, it often has less to do with a real-life baby than with a metaphorical one. Dreams of this nature may be a reference to the "inner child," or the "baby" within, or even to a part of yourself that longs to be reborn anew. Did you witness a difficult birth in your dream? If so, and you're not actually pregnant, could this relate to an idea you're laboring to realize or a project you're trying to get off the ground? Or could you be trying to rediscover an aspect of your personality that has been dormant recently?

A DREAM BIRTH

If you are a pregnant woman who dreamed of giving birth, your dream was a reflection of your hopes and fears with regard to your impending due date. But if you're not pregnant, this dream probably represented a new beginning of some kind, or a chance to start again. Such dreams become more common as we age, even beyond the menopause.

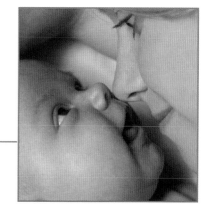

THE LIFE CYCLE

Related themes:
Adolescence
School
Family members

CHILDHOOD

In dreamland, a child, whether or not it is you, almost always represents the child within—usually the carefree young innocent that you once were and, perhaps, would like to be again. Dreams in which a child (or a childhood symbol, such as a toy) plays a leading role may indicate that your waking responsibilities are troubling you. Is it time to restore the balance by allowing yourself to have some fun, or to adopt a simpler, less adult, perspective on life? Alternatively, such dreams may be alerting you to your childish or selfish behavior in the real world. Ask yourself whether you should "grow up" and handle things maturely.

FUN AND GAMES

Did you dream of a carefree child who was playing outdoors, having fun and laughing in delight? And could the child have been you? If you are experiencing a lot of pressure in your working life, or as a carer, dreams such as this may act as a safety valve, allowing you subconsciously to "let go" and liberate yourself (briefly) from your waking responsibilities.

THE LIFE CYCLE

Related themes:
Childhood
Embarrassment
Coming of Age

ADOLESCENCE

The appearance of adolescents in dreams may have less to do with innocence and powerlessness and more to do with youthful attitudes and behavior as well as the choices that teenagers face when they are about to cross the threshold from childhood into the adult world. Are your teen years long gone, yet you dreamed of being transported back in time, regaining your youthful looks and outlook? If so, you may be mourning the loss of precisely those qualities as a consequence of aging, or you may be regretting not having made the most of your potential and the opportunities that beckoned at a time when the world was your oyster.

FIRST KISS

If you dreamed of your first kiss, or of teenagers whom you don't know experiencing the thrill of their first kiss, is your love life becoming less than exciting? Perhaps you need to think of ways to put some of the electricity back into your relationship before it becomes too stale; or perhaps your subconscious has detected that your partner is losing interest, and this dream was a warning.

THE LIFE CYCLE

Related themes:
Adolescence
Starting a new job
Graduation

COMING OF AGE

There is no single event upon which we enter adulthood; we are given freedoms and responsibilities in small increments, and these milestones have varying degrees of significance for different people. Did you have a dream in which you relived some moment from your past that you felt ushered you into your adult life? Perhaps it was the first time you stood up to your father, or the day you moved into your first apartment? If so, it is likely that your unconscious mind summoned this memory in order to remind you that it is once again time to take initiative and to "stand on your own two feet" in the world.

MILESTONES

Did you dream of learning to drive, or did you relive in your dream the first time you were allowed to ride a motorbike? If your dream centered on a "grown up" activity that you were secretly afraid of trying as a teenager, perhaps your remembered sense of pride in confronting that fear reflects your feelings about a new endeavor in your waking world today.

SELF & OTHERS

Related themes:
Childbirth
Mother
Pride

THE LIFE CYCLE

PREGNANCIES

If you are either pregnant or trying to conceive, dreaming of carrying a baby may reflect your actual situation and your hopes and fears. Otherwise, the dream may have been fulfilling your profound yearnings for a baby. If procreation in the real world is not on your mind, however, then perhaps your dream relates to your inner "baby"—an aspect of yourself that is dependent on others for emotional or physical sustenance, or a part of yourself that longs to be given life or to be reborn. Could your gestating dream baby symbolize your "brainchild," a project that you have conceived and are developing until it is ready for the wider world?

UNWELCOME NEWS?
An apprehensive reaction in a dream in which you find yourself pregnant may reflect your waking uncertainty about the possibility of conceiving. It could be, for instance, that your partner wants to start a family, while you're not so sure. If you were horrified by your dream conception, it may be that you really don't want a baby, but you fear that you've conceived accidentally.

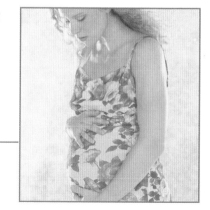

THE LIFE CYCLE

Related themes:
Pregnancy
Hospital
Family members

CHILDBIRTH

Are you an expectant mother who dreamed of going into labor? If so, and your dream labor was difficult, the dream simply reflects your inevitable anxieties, and your unconscious may have put you through this unpleasant dummy run in order to force you to confront your fears, preparing you for the testing event ahead. Or did you dream of having a baby, but aren't actually a prospective or aspiring parent? If so, perhaps the birthing process denotes the imminent entrance of a fully formed idea, plan, or project into your real-life world—something that will no longer be a figment of your imagination, but will have a life of its own, while your own life will never be the same again.

A NEW ARRIVAL?

If you dreamed that you gave birth to a healthy, happy baby, yet you are not pregnant in the real world, could the new arrival have represented a project that you have been developing—one that should be coming to fruition soon? This dream reveals your subconscious confidence that the "brainchild" or project is ready to enter the world successfully.

THE LIFE CYCLE

Related themes:
Health, sickness, death
Grandparents
Wise woman, witch, magician or wizard archetypes

OLD AGE

When our unconscious mind places an older person at the forefront of our dreams, it may do so in order to highlight qualities like experience, wisdom, and kindness, or it may reflect our real-world anxieties about aging, our own mortality, or the well-being of an elderly relative. Did you know the person? If it was one of your grandparents, his or her presence in your dream may have filled you with a feeling of happy nostalgia, or could have represented an archetypal figure with a message to impart. Or were you the old person, perhaps enjoying a relaxed retirement from the stresses of your waking world, or else feeling sick and fearing that your best years are behind you?

SITTING BACK

In your dream, did you watch as a contented older person enjoyed a leisurely afternoon, perhaps watching a grandchild playing, or simply taking the air? And did you then realize that the older person was actually you? This dream could be the expression of a suppressed wish that you could take a rest from your waking responsibilities and enjoy a well-earned rest, at least for a while.

THE LIFE CYCLE

Related themes:
Loneliness, grief
Funerals
Endings or change

DEATHS

For most of us, dreams that involve death are among the most disturbing. When our unconscious mind brings death to our attention, however, there are many possible interpretations, more often symbolic than literal. If you dreamed of the death of a loved one who is quite well in the real world, perhaps he or she represented some part of your life that you would like to bring to an end. Unless you are terminally ill, then a dream that highlights your own death is highly unlikely to portend your actual demise. You may be anxious about your health or seeking an "escape" from the world; or facing a life change that you are about to make (which is a sort of metaphorical death, but also a new beginning).

THE GRIM REAPER
Did you awake sweating from a nightmare in which you were stalked by the Grim Reaper, with his threatening scythe? If so, and you are not suffering from a serious illness in real life, it is likely that you fear an impending change in the real world, one that will mean the "death" of a familiar routine?

SELF & OTHERS

Related themes:
Pregnancy
Childbirth
Festivals and parties

RITES OF PASSAGE

NAMING CEREMONIES

In your dream, did you attend an infant's naming ceremony or baptism? If so, and you have no such waking-life events on the horizon, perhaps the baby who was being named or baptized in your dream represents a concept or idea that is about to be formally presented to a new audience. Perhaps you have been considering setting up your own company; your unconscious may be telling you that the time is right to put your plans into action. Or perhaps your dream denoted your wish either to be "reborn" yourself, or for someone else to undergo a transformation that would redirect him or her down the right path in life.

BABY BAPTISM

A dream of an old-fashioned, ritualistic naming ceremony that was very formal (perhaps even recalling an earlier era) was probably connected with your subconscious desire for a transformation or for a public "cleansing" to "wash away" your recent misdemeanors or unhealthy or self-destructive behavior. If the dream baby represented a loved one, could that person be in need of redemption?

RITES OF PASSAGE

Related themes:
Death, grief
Transformations
Being buried alive

FUNERALS

In the realm of the unconscious, funerals share the various interpretations associated with dreams of death and dying (see previous pages), so it may be helpful to ask yourself if worries about your health are preying on your mind; if there's anything in your life or character that you long to "lay to rest"; or whether a dream funeral (particularly if it wasn't yours) could have represented a relationship that you'd like to bring to an end. Were you surprised to find yourself observing your own funeral service, gathering, or wake in your dream, but rather than feeling sad or regretful, was your overriding emotion curiosity about what would be said about you? Who were the mourners in your dream, and were you gratified and validated by what they said?

DEAD AND BURIED
Was it a burial that you witnessed in your dream? If so, whether it was you or someone else who was being interred, your unconscious may have been trying to signal that a life phase is about to be "dead and buried," or else that you wish that something you are finding highly problematic in your life could be.

SELF & OTHERS

Related themes:
Lovers
Wish fulfillment
Love, happiness

RITES OF PASSAGE

WEDDINGS

Dreaming of a wedding may have temporarily fulfilled your waking matrimonial wishes (or else emphasized your doubts about making such a lifelong commitment), but other interpretations may be more relevant to your current situation. Your unconscious mind may have used the wedding as a metaphor for an entirely different form of commitment— one that is unromantic in the extreme, such as your commitment to your career or to a financial obligation. Did you find yourself pledging your troth, for better or for worse, to a bride or bridegroom in front of a moist-eyed congregation in your dream? How did you feel as you uttered those solemn wedding vows, and to whom did you make them?

WEDDED BLISS

If you are actually engaged to be married, or else wish that you were (and, on waking, longed for your dream to come true), your unconscious may have been indulging you in dreamland by depicting your heartfelt hopes. Were you jumping for joy in your bridal wear? Or was your dream bride or groom the person you daydream of marrying?

RITES OF PASSAGE

SELF & OTHERS

Related themes:
Betrayal
Loss, death
Fear, loneliness

DIVORCES

Dreams of unfaithfulness and divorce can be deeply unsettling, particularly if you believe your relationship to be rock solid in real life. You may be relieved, therefore, to know that these dreams may not reflect the actual state of your marriage or relationship. Instead, your unconscious may have been bringing to the fore anxious, guilty, or escapist feelings—emotions that, again, may not refer to your romantic or domestic situation at all, but to a platonic friendship or professional association. If your marriage has actually hit a rocky patch, you have grown apart emotionally, or your sex life has become moribund, a dream of divorcing may have made your unconscious yearnings manifest, underlining your dissatisfaction with the state of your marriage.

"SEE YOU IN COURT!"

If your dream featured you and your partner in a cold, clinical meeting in a courtroom or lawyer's office, perhaps your waking-life feelings for him or her have seriously cooled off. Are you suppressing the suspicion that he or she is having an affair, or are you secretly contemplating one?

RITES OF PASSAGE

Related themes:
New beginnings
Being uprepared
Fear, frustration

STARTING SCHOOL

Did you dream that you had become a child again—one who felt lost, lonely, and bewildered because your dream portrayed you on your first day at school? If so, have you recently started a new job or moved to a different area? The unconscious often draws on past experiences to reflect how we are currently feeling, and your reaction to your dramatic change of circumstances may have mirrored a childhood trauma of finding yourself in a new environment, among strangers, unsure of how to behave, and worried about what's expected of you and how others regard you. Dreams like these may occur when a childhood insecurity about being judged by your peers, along with a related fear of being unpopular, or even shunned, are aroused in the waking world.

HAPPY DAYS
A dream in which you ran happily into school for your first day, taking your place at your new desk with eager anticipation, may signify that you are keen to make changes in your waking life, or perhaps that you wish you could revert back to a former situation in which you were happier and more carefree.

RITES OF PASSAGE

SELF & OTHERS

Related themes:
Success
Celebrations
New beginnings

GRADUATING SCHOOL OR UNIVERSITY

We all have ambitions, be they personal or professional, and when we dream of achieving a goal and accepting recognition for it, as on a graduation day, the dream may express simple wish fulfillment. But did you dream that you were graduating from school or college but felt reluctant to leave, to say goodbye to your fellow students, and to move on to a new phase of life? If so, perhaps you are unsettled in your waking life by the prospect of having to take on more responsibilities or independence—or simply to face up to change. The key to interpreting dreams like these is to work out how you were feeling in the dream, and why.

SUCCESS!

If your dream featured you jumping for joy with your fellow graduates as you accepted congratulations for your hard work and achievement, was your unconscious reminding you that you should feel proud of yourself? Have you recently gained success in some field of your life, perhaps achieving a promotion at work? Or was your dream the fulfillment of a wish to obtain recognition from others?

Related themes:
Insecurity
Being judged
Being unprepared

RITES OF PASSAGE

INTERVIEWS, BEING HIRED & FIRED

If you dreamed of being nervous in an interview or audition, it is likely to have been a fear-of-failure dream, carrying the threat of being judged and found inadequate by your inquisitor(s). Do you have an interview, presentation, or performance looming that is making you anxious in real life? If not, could the boss or director in your dream have represented a despotic teacher who tormented you many years ago? Perhaps, on the other hand, you sailed through your interview and were congratulated by an admiring panel, and offered a job or promotion. This was probably a wish-fulfillment dream or an unconscious confidence boost.

"YOU'RE HIRED!"

Interviews are stressful situations in which we put ourselves on show for someone else to judge our worth. If you dreamed of handling yourself with confidence, impressing your interviewer, and being awarded the job on the spot, your unconscious may have been indicating that you are ready for a new challenge and that you're worth more than you are currently being recognized for at work.

RITES OF PASSAGE

Related themes:
Being unprepared
Teachers
Fear

TESTS & EXAMS

Did you dream of taking an exam, and if so, are you a student in real life? And were you confident and prepared for the dream test, or did you draw a blank and panic at the incomprehensible paper? The latter sort of dream usually highlights a waking anxiety about failing a test or challenge that you are facing in your life—perhaps you literally need to study harder, or maybe your challenge concerns your work, if you are not a student. Were you suddenly being singled out and put on the spot by a dream teacher? Your unconscious mind may be reminding you of humiliations you suffered at school; but perhaps you rose to the challenge, unlike during your schooldays.

TESTING TIMES
Dreaming of taking an exam is often a reflection of your self-esteem; the key to interpreting the dream is how you felt during the exam. If you were untroubled by the test questions and came up with creative, clever, and original answers, your dream suggests that your self-confidence is high, whether or not you have tests looming in the waking world.

SELF & OTHERS

Related themes:
Authority figures
Archetypes, animus
Emotional security

FAMILY MEMBERS

FATHERS

Most of us become gradually less reliant on our parents as we tread the path toward adulthood, yet vestiges of our early emotional dependency remain with us. And because our parents wielded such enormous influence over us, our feelings toward them remain intense. Did you dream that your father chided you about your recent performance at work, and do you have uncomfortable memories of him admonishing you for not studying harder at school or for poor grades? If so, your dream may be underlining your own dissatisfaction at not having met the standards that your father instilled in you. When your dream parents are true to their actual characters, the message can be taken at face value.

FANTASY FATHER

In your dream, did a loving father-figure praise and encourage you, yet you grew up without a father, or else your father was distant or critical of you? If so, your unconscious may have invoked the archetype of an ideal father to make up for the lack of this role in your life. For example, your dream father may symbolize protection from a real threat.

FAMILY MEMBERS

Related themes:
Childhood
Grandmother
Parenthood

MOTHERS

The dreams that you have of your mother may have many interpretations, ranging from straightforward to complex. All, however, hinge on how you perceive your emotional interaction with her, particularly when you were a child. Did your dreaming mind cast your emotionally withdrawn mother as an angel of compassion? Dreams in which parents behave out of character can be unsettling. Such dreams may have more to do with unresolved aspects of yourself or your life situation that you have never fully (if at all) acknowledged or addressed, but perhaps need to in order to find emotional peace or fulfillment.

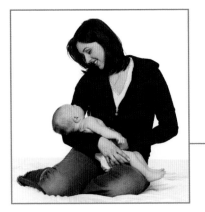

MATERNAL EMBRACE
Did your mother appear in your dream to give you a comforting hug and words of encouragement, and was she warm and loving toward you while you were growing up? If so, your dream may simply be confirming the importance of the maternal role that she has played in your life, perhaps also indicating that you are feeling insecure and in need of some validation and unconditional love.

SELF & OTHERS

FAMILY MEMBERS

Related themes:
Childhood
Rivalry
Emotional support

BROTHERS & SISTERS

Our interaction with our siblings is usually less burdened by the search for individuality and independence that often complicates our relationships with our parents. That having been said, the conflict engendered by sibling rivalry frequently looms large between brothers and sisters. And although this conflict typically lessens as the years pass, vestiges of childhood jealousy may resurface in the dream world. A dream in which your brother or sister is cast in a negative light may, therefore, denote unresolved and corrosive childhood feelings toward that sibling. If your bullying brother tormented you in your dream, is it time to stand up to him now?

SIBLING TOGETHERNESS

Are you an only child, yet your dream featured you playing with a brother or sister? Such dreams of sibling situations that have no mirror in the waking world may have nothing to do with family, but instead point to an aspect of yourself. In this example, do you need support to help you deal with something stressful, or time out from work or family commitments to "play" or relax?

FAMILY MEMBERS

Related themes:
Love
Emotional security
Betrayal

HUSBANDS & WIVES

Dreaming of a spouse can have many different meanings, depending on both your real-life situation and how you felt in the dream. Did you wake up shocked from a dream in which you caught your husband of ten years in bed with another woman? A dream like this usually just reflects your insecurity about the constancy of your partner's love for you, although you may indeed be feeling threatened (even if needlessly)—perhaps by a female colleague who's started working in his office, and whom he clearly admires. Your dreaming mind may have portrayed your worst-case scenario to prepare you to confront, and deal with, your fears.

TOGETHERNESS

If you are happily married and dreamed of a cozy lie-in with your spouse, your dream merely reflects your intimate relationship. But were you divorced many years ago in real life? Or are you shocked to realize that your dream spouse was actually your friend's husband? Try to examine your true feelings: do you need to deal with your loneliness, or are you attracted to someone "off limits"?

SELF & OTHERS

FAMILY MEMBERS

Related themes:
Childhood
Siblings
Parents

SONS & DAUGHTERS

Many parents are deeply intuitive where their children are concerned, although this may be on a more unconscious than conscious level. If you are a parent, the most likely explanation for any dream that features your child is therefore a straightforward one. If you dreamed that your son was in danger, for example, it simply means that you are worried about his safety. Equally, a dream in which your daughter accuses you of not understanding her indicates that your unconscious mind has become aware that you have been brushing aside her opinions and that you should perhaps try harder to see certain issues from her point of view.

HAPPY FAMILIES

If you dreamed that you were a parent, but you are actually childless, your dream was probably a form of wish fulfillment, especially if you are trying to conceive in real life (or else uncomfortably aware that your "body clock" is ticking loudly). Or, your dream offspring may represent archetypes that could reflect an aspect of yourself, or else be relevant to your current situation.

FAMILY MEMBERS

Related themes:
Jealousy
Parents
Rivals

IN-LAWS & STEPFAMILIES

Dreams about in-laws and stepfamily can reflect your waking circumstances if they are about actual family members, but their meaning will be much more cryptic if the dream characters are not people in your daily life. If your young children are spending a lot of time with your ex and his or her new partner, dreaming of them as a happy family unit—without you—is a simple reflection of your waking fears that you'll lose their affections. (You won't!) Or are you a stepmother to sullen teenagers, and did you awake shocked after dreaming (gleefully) that your stepchildren moved away to live with relatives in another country? Such dreams simply help to relieve the intense pressures of stepfamily life.

STRANGERS AT MY TABLE

Did you awake disconcerted from a dream in which you attended a family celebration, only to discover that you had step-siblings that no one had told you about? Such dreams reveal feelings of insecurity, either in your own identity, or in the state of your relationships with the people in your dream. Have you become distant from your parents lately?

Related themes:
Wisdom
Experience
Emotional security

FAMILY MEMBERS

GRANDPARENTS

Apart from reflecting a nostalgic yearning for the security of childhood and tight-knit familial bonds, dreaming of either of your grandparents may indicate that you are unconsciously crying out for their loving guidance, born of a lifetime's experience, as you dodge your way past life's dilemmas and pitfalls. But if you don't associate the grandparent of whom you dreamed with a reliable source of wisdom, ask yourself whether he or she could have been an archetype in disguise, especially the priestess (or wise old woman) or priest (or wise old man). Whoever you identify your dream grandparent as, heeding the advice he or she has given will help to set you on the path that is right for you.

IN LOCO PARENTIS?

If you regarded your grandparents as people on whom you could always rely for unconditional affection (particularly if your relationship with your parents was fraught), their appearance in your dreams may be reassuring. Your dream grandparent may have appeared to remind you of the happy times that you shared, or to impart a specific message of encouragement or advice.

PROFESSIONAL & AUTHORITY FIGURES

SELF & OTHERS

Related themes:
Father figures
Violence
Conscience

POLICE OFFICERS

When police appear in our dreams, they may do so as the voice of our conscience, reminding us to do what we have been taught is right, or upbraiding us for misbehaving. Alternatively, they may be advisors and guides, helping us to see the most appropriate course of action when we are unsure of ourselves; or else they may symbolize power, whether benign or otherwise. The authority of policemen as upholders of the rule of state and law of the land is symbolized by the depersonalizing uniform that they wear. The very presence of a uniformed character in our dreams can be alarming or reassuring, depending on the situation.

WAKE-UP CALL

Did you dream that a police car drew up beside you as you walked along a city street, and did an officer look at you as if to question your behavior or ask where you were headed? If so, do you have a guilty conscience about something you have been doing, or planning to do, in your waking life, perhaps deluding yourself that you can get away with it when, deep down, you know it is wrong?

PROFESSIONAL & AUTHORITY FIGURES

Related themes:
Police
Guilt
Father figures

LAWYERS

In your dream, did you tremble in front of a judge as he sternly passed sentence upon you? Dreams of being tried and found guilty often express the feeling that you deserve, at some level, to be punished for something that you've either done or contemplated doing. Your unconscious may be warning you not to continue with your "crime," which, in the waking world, could be something quite trivial, like forgetting your mother's birthday. But if you knew that you were innocent and yet still judged to be in the wrong, your unconscious may have been reflecting your waking sense of grievance at having been "misjudged" over something.

GUILTY AS CHARGED!

In your dream, did you play the part of judge yourself, declaring your verdict on the behavior of someone in your waking life who has transgressed against you in some way? This may simply reflect a real scenario in which you have been wronged; it may even be a kind of wish-fulfillment if you would dearly like to have the power to prevent and condemn someone's abusive behavior.

PROFESSIONAL & AUTHORITY FIGURES

SELF & OTHERS

Related themes:
Mother or father figures
Confidence
Childhood

TEACHERS

Aside from your parents, teachers were probably the first authority figures to wield power over you. Because you were subject to their control at a deeply impressionable age, the stamp of their authority may have remained imprinted on your mind, later emerging in your dreams as a mentor or tormentor. If you dreamed of a teacher whom you feared and hated when you were at school because he or she was sadistic or picked on you, is your current boss making your waking life hell by persecuting you? Or do you feel insecure about a project you've been working on, and did your dream teacher expose you to ridicule and humiliation?

MENTOR/PROTECTOR

If you dreamed that a maternal, kindly teacher was presiding over a kindergarten class, were you the teacher or one of the children? If you were a child, perhaps your dream teacher represents someone who can protect or help you in your waking life. If you were the teacher, is there someone you know who depends upon you as a mentor or advocate and who needs and values your support?

PROFESSIONAL & AUTHORITY FIGURES

Related themes:
Insecurity
Power and authority
Teachers

BOSSES & SUPERVISORS

In archetypal terms, your boss in a dream might have been a manifestation of the ogre, the cruel face of authority, who uses power unjustly and demands submission. But perhaps your real boss is nothing like the person in your dream: could this ruthless tyrant have been pointing to your own tendency to treat your subordinates with ruthless harshness? Or perhaps your dream boss was not authoritarian, but someone willing and able to take on responsibilities and burdens, possibly leaving you feeling liberated of some of the pressure you have been feeling recently.

POWER GAMES

In your dream, did a younger person usurp your rightful place of seniority and condemn you to a junior role, and did he or she refuse to take any notice of your ideas? Do you feel insecure or inadequate at your workplace, or else is someone new to your organization threatening your position there? If you had a dream like this, take time to consider whether you may benefit from training or coaching to refresh your skills and restore your self-confidence.

PROFESSIONAL & AUTHORITY FIGURES

Related themes:
The body
Ageing
Health and well-being

DOCTORS & DENTISTS

When professionals and authority figures appear in dreams, their significance is probably related to their area of expertise. If your dream depicted a doctor taking your blood pressure, for instance, was your unconscious telling you that your stress levels are too high and that you need to address issues in your lifestyle and level of commitments? If the doctor pronounced that you are sick, your unconscious may have been warning you of a malaise affecting your emotional well-being, or perhaps, in waking life, you have been worrying excessively about a symptom that you need to have checked out. Take heed of the dream doctor's words.

OPEN WIDE!

If you dreamed that you were in the dentist's chair being told that you were losing your teeth, you experienced a classic anxiety dream, which may well have been related to a change that is affecting your waking circumstances. Or, are you worried about ageing or losing your looks, or do you simply need to be reminded by your unconscious that your regular dental check-up is due?

STRANGERS & ARCHETYPES

Related themes:
Lover
Stranger
Femme fatale

DON JUAN & CASANOVA FIGURES

The appearance of a philanderer or seducer in your dreams may be your unconscious mind's way of warning you to beware of an archetypal wastrel, someone who tempts you to misbehave—perhaps, but not always, sexually—and does not have your interests at heart. Have you recently come under the spell of a beguiling newcomer to your workplace or social scene, and should you look more carefully at his motives and behavior? Another explanation for this type of dream character is that he might represent your animus, if you are a woman. Are you too sexually submissive, and might this dream suggest that you take the initiative?

SEDUCTION

In your dream, were you mesmerized by an attractive stranger who charmed you to bed without a moment's thought to your real-life relationship? Such dreams are a harmless expression of sexual yearnings that most of us harbor, consciously or not. Or perhaps you are a man who dreamed of an exciting male lover: was your dream a reflection of your true, but repressed, sexual identity?

STRANGERS & ARCHETYPES

Related themes:
Lover
Stranger
Sexuality

FEMMES FATALES

The female equivalent of the wastrel archetype is the siren or seductress, who leads men to their doom, powerless in the face of her attractiveness or sexual appetite. If you are a man who dreamed of being ensnared by a sexually predatory woman, could this have simply been wish-fulfillment, especially if you have been celibate for too long? Or could the vamp have been your anima—a reflection of your feminine side—and did she appear in your dream to remind you not to neglect your need for an intimate sexual relationship? If so, perhaps you have been working too hard of late and should concentrate on getting out more.

FATAL ATTRACTION?

Did you dream that you were singled out by a woman who was determined to seduce you, and did you tumble helpless into her arms? If so, and you are already involved with a woman, this dream need not have a literal interpretation about infidelity. The reverse could even be true, if your dream left you with the feeling that you should behave more maturely than to be led by easy temptation.

STRANGERS & ARCHETYPES

Related themes:
Bad behavior
Irresponsibility
Shock and horror

THE SHADOW

If you awoke from a dream that featured someone of the same gender as you who behaved in a way that you found shocking or loathsome, and your instinctive response to the person was to recoil, you may have encountered your archetypal shadow. This figure has the opposite characteristics to those of the persona that your ego has carefully constructed. He or she represents the dark, hidden side of your psyche and embodies all the traits that you do not want to acknowledge in yourself. While you might not like to believe yourself capable of the behavior or thoughts that your shadow displayed, these may well be latent in you.

THE DARK SIDE

In your dream, did someone act spitefully toward a vulnerable person, and then proceed to humiliate the victim by rubbing his or her nose in the situation? It could just be that the perpetrator of this nastiness was your shadow, and you might recognize the meanness in your long-buried childhood memories of bullying a less confident child. If so, forgive your childhood self and move on.

STRANGERS & ARCHETYPES

Related themes:
Money problems
Loyalty
Loneliness

HOMELESS PEOPLE

Dream beggars and vagrants may appear in order to caution you that unless you change some aspect of your life, you, too, could lose everything and end up tramping the streets. While such dream characters may warn of impending monetary losses—perhaps even bankruptcy—this meaning is generally only pertinent if your financial situation in the real world is giving you cause for concern. Was the homeless person you, or someone close to you, or was he or she a stranger? If it was you, yet you are not in a precarious financial situation, maybe you fear becoming impoverished in another sense—emotionally or creatively, for example.

EASY STREET
In your dream, did you see an old friend in the guise of a down-and-out panhandler, and did you avert your eyes as you hurried by? Such a dream could indicate that your recent career successes have left you too preoccupied to pay attention to important relationships that cannot be neglected any longer. Does someone in your waking life need your help, and have you turned the other cheek?

STRANGERS & ARCHETYPES

Related themes:
Wealth
The body
Achievement

CELEBRITIES

When we see images of famous people, we may fleetingly imagine being like those visions of extraordinary beauty (if we are women) or those celebrated icons of manliness (if we are men). The same holds true if a celebrity graced your dream with their stellar presence. Whether you unconsciously yearn to be as good-looking, rich, or powerful as the star who descended from unattainable heights into your dream world, or whether you would simply love to bed them, such dreams are frequently the wish-fulfilling response of your unconscious to your desires. Dreams like these could reflect insecurities about ageing or dating.

LIGHTS, CAMERA, ACTION!

A dream in which you starred as a glamorous character with fabulous riches and success may point up your dissatisfaction with your current circumstances, or perhaps your lack of self-esteem. Do you daydream of being beautiful or wealthy, but your reality is far from this? If so, work on boosting your self-esteem, while thinking through changes you could make in your life.

STRANGERS & ARCHETYPES

Related themes:
Sabotage
Unpredictability
Egotism

CLOWNS & TRICKSTERS

The archetypal trickster represents that part of your unconscious self that feels—often justifiably—obliged to sabotage your most earnest conscious efforts. Clowning around, throwing insults, unpredictable behavior, and shape-shifting are all hallmarks of the trickster. This wild, egotistical side of yourself may encourage you to do things you'd never imagine doing, even if you secretly want to. So if you dreamed of a clown, or of someone playing tricks and acting the fool, could it have been the archetypal trickster, and do you need a good dose of shaking up, lightening up, or taking down a peg or two? Trying acting on your impulses, for once.

TEARS OF A CLOWN

Dreaming of a clown face that is clearly painted over an unhappy or stressed expression indicates that the dream clown is putting on a show. Was it you, or someone you know? And are you (or he or she) trying to conceal your misery behind a brave facade? Alternatively, perhaps the clown was attempting to cheer up an onlooker who has been having a rough time lately.

Related themes:
Spouses
Fidelity
Betrayal

FRIENDS & LOVERS

LOVERS

The sexual urge is powerful enough to explain the fact that we so frequently have explicitly sexual dreams. This is especially true during adolescence, when hormones cause havoc and fuel the sexual curiosity that is a hallmark of this life stage. We may dream of ourselves with actual lovers, fantasy lovers, or even people whom we can't stand in real life. So if you dreamed that you had a passionate encounter with someone you can barely bring yourself to speak to, or else with someone of your own gender (if you are heterosexual), you probably awoke feeling horrified. Don't attach too much significance to it, though: instead, think of it as exploration, wish fulfillment, or frustration, as appropriate.

LOVE AND WAR
Did you awake disturbed and feeling emotionally fragile because you had dreamed of fighting or breaking off with your real-life lover? Such dreams can be upsetting but do not necessarily prefigure a serious rift in real life. Instead, ask yourself whether you have buried fears about your relationship, and, if so, are they justified? Can you work on the issues together?

FRIENDS & LOVERS

Related themes:
Stress
Childhood
Emotional security

COLLEAGUES & CLASSMATES

Interaction with others is an essential aspect of being at school or college and of almost any job. Your dream of either colleagues or classmates may therefore have been drawing a parallel with how well you relate to your colleagues during your waking hours. But did you dream of finding yourself in a new environment, among strangers, unsure of how to behave, and worried about the impression you make on others? If so, and you haven't recently changed jobs or started college, you may simply be remembering a childhood insecurity about being judged as inadequate by your peers, along with a related fear of being unpopular or seen as "uncool."

A HARD DAY'S NIGHT

In your dream, were you at work with your real-life colleagues, and have you been working too hard recently, or else do you have a particularly stressful problem to resolve, or deadline to meet, or working relationship that needs improving? When you can't let go of work as you leave your workplace for the day, it is not uncommon to dream about the issues that are on your mind.

SELF & OTHERS

FRIENDS & LOVERS

Related themes:
Betrayal
Family
Parties

FRIENDS

Did you dream about your best friend, whom you see often? If so, and if he or she behaved or communicated with you in the same easy manner that characterizes your relationship in the waking world, it's safe to assume that the dream merely reflects the important part that he or she plays in your life. A similar interpretation applies if your friend has moved away and face-to-face contact is rare, and such a dream may also remind you that a reunion or communication may be long overdue. Nightmares involving friends, on the other hand, may signify that your relationship is not all that it seems, and if your friend's dream behavior was troubling, it may even be time to break the friendship off.

THREE'S A CROWD
Have you recently made a new friend in your waking world, and has he or she begun to enter your wider social circle? If you dreamed that your new friend was becoming a little too friendly for your liking, or getting between you and your more long-standing friends, or your partner, are you worried that he or she poses a threat to you in the real world?

MIND & BODY

When you dream of a particular part of the body, you may have had the same subject at the forefront of your waking mind—for example, a neckache, or a new hairstyle. But these dreams can be metaphors, too, so that a dream of having both legs amputated probably refers to a sudden loss of independence, freedom, or control in the real world. Dreams involving powerful emotions, on the other hand, are often safety-valve experiences (as, for example, when we dream of having an angry exchange with an in-law, whereas in real life such an expression of feeling would be unthinkable). Or, they may temporarily fulfill our deepest wishes or fears.

MIND & BODY

Related themes:
Freedom
Love
Wish fulfillment

POSITIVE EMOTIONS

HAPPINESS

If, in your dream, you felt full of happiness or warm contentment, and if this characterizes your overall response to the world around you when you're awake, you can count yourself lucky! More likely, however, you have doubts or worries about aspects of your work and relationships. If something is bothering you, yet your dreaming self luxuriated in rosy feelings, perhaps your unconscious mind was trying to hearten you and enhance your sense of well-being in compensation for your conscious unhappiness. Alternatively, your unconscious may have given you clues through the medium of dreams on how to find happiness in your life.

TOP OF THE WORLD!

If you were jumping for joy in your dream, was the dream situation something that you consciously yearn for? This is a classic wish-fulfillment dream. If, however, the source of your dream happiness was not something you want, could there be a hidden clue to something that could make you happier? If, for instance, you dreamed of enjoying a fairground ride, could the message simply be that you need to have more fun?

POSITIVE EMOTIONS

Related themes:
Freedom
Confidence
Emotional security

RELIEF & LIBERATION

Occasionally, a dream may give us such an exhilarating sense of release, liberation, or freedom, that waking up to the realization that it was just a dream comes as a bit of a disappointment. Do you feel that the limitations of your life have pushed you into a corner from which you can't escape? Are you feeling trapped in an unhappy relationship, or do you feel that you'll never find a soulmate, or are others sapping your energy or stifling your individuality? If so, a relief or liberation dream may provide the clue to a way out of your situation: when you can find the strength, the route to real-life liberation is probably in your own hands.

BREAKING FREE

If you are currently being controlled or limited by someone—an authority figure such as your father, teacher, or boss, or perhaps someone with whom you have a dysfunctional relationship—your dream of breaking free from the situation should be seen as a stimulus to take steps to move on, somehow, with your life. What practical steps can you take to follow up your dream of freedom?

MIND & BODY

Related themes:
Husband/wife
Lovers
Family relationships

POSITIVE EMOTIONS

LOVE

In your dream, did you feel passionate love for someone? The most important step to take when interpreting your dream is to ask yourself who, or what, aroused such feelings in you. If it was your partner, whom you adore, your dream is simply underlining your feelings for him or her. If, however, things are not so straightforward between you, it may be that your dreaming mind is reminding you of the overwhelming love that you once felt, and could quickly rekindle. But if you dreamed that you were in love with someone else, is that person off limits to you in life because of your own, or his or her, relationship with another?

THAT LOVIN' FEELING

If you dreamed that you were locked in a warm and happy embrace with someone you actually desire in the waking world, your dream was a simple wish fulfillment. But if, on the other hand, you saw the object of your desire in the arms of someone else, your level of self-esteem may be low, and you should try to work on boosting your confidence and sense of self-worth.

POSITIVE EMOTIONS

Related themes:
Winning
Wish fulfillment
Popularity

SUCCESS

Whether you dreamed of receiving a Nobel prize, graduating with an honors degree, coming first in a competition, or winning the attentions of someone you admire while your rival could only look on enviously, the unconscious mind was providing you with a boost to your confidence, or else heartening you if your current circumstances are not quite so flushed with achievement or good luck. Such dreams are a common response to feelings of being under-recognized or taken for granted. They can also occur if your waking focus is fixed on achieving something in particular. On the other hand, if you've been slacking lately, a dream like this could simply point up what you may be missing.

HIGH ESTEEM

Did you dream that someone whose opinion you value was congratulating you warmly on a recent success? And is the person in your dream actually someone who rarely pays attention to you? This dream may mean that you crave validation from others, but your subconscious was pointing out that you should boost your own sense of self-worth.

NEGATIVE EMOTIONS

Related themes:
Grief
Loss
Nostalgia

SADNESS

Dreams can be a useful outlet for negative emotions that we try to keep at bay during daily life. If, in your dream, you were swamped with sadness and you wept uncontrollably, it is likely that you have indeed had cause for grief in waking life, but that you have buried your feelings rather than put yourself through the pain of working them through, or you are waiting for the passage of time to work its healing magic. You may have found that shedding floods of dream tears was cathartic, and you may have woken feeling melancholy, yet also unburdened. If you constantly find yourself crying and stricken with unhappiness in your dreams, however, your unconscious may be giving expression to your general state of depression, and you should seek help.

BLUE MOODS

If you awoke from a dream with a sense of overwhelming melancholy, can you pinpoint what made you sad in your dream? Your unconscious was probably highlighting a real cause of sadness and giving vent to your unhappiness to help you move on, especially if you have been repressing your feelings.

NEGATIVE EMOTIONS

Related themes:
Death
Endings (of a phase or project)
The "empty nest"

GRIEF

Dreams of losing people we love are not uncommon. If, in the real world, you have recently lost a family member or someone close to you, you should be aware of the likelihood of reliving your initial grief and desolation for some time in dreamland, because this is part of the process of coming to terms with loss. These dreams can also be cathartic experiences because they allow us to express our grief, and perhaps anger, more graphically than we feel able to in the real world (particularly if we fear upsetting those around us). However, if you dreamed that you were grieving for someone who is alive and well, are you doing anything to create distance between you in the waking world?

DEATH THROES

In your dream, did you see your mother, lover, or best friend weeping by an empty hospital bed, and were you the person who had died? Dreaming of one's own death need not signal anything alarming. The unconscious uses imagery like this to remind us of how much we are valued by people around us, even if they don't always show it.

MIND & BODY

Related themes:
Abandonment
Shyness
Lack of confidence

NEGATIVE EMOTIONS

LONELINESS

Feelings of loneliness are not confined to those who are isolated in their current time and place in life. If, for example, you are married, but your spouse is focused exclusively on work and you feel deprived of affection, feelings of loneliness may surface during your sleep (for example, you may dream of being a widow or widower). Perhaps your dream focused on an emotional distance that resulted from a sudden argument, but that, if left unresolved, could end up being a permanent rift. But what if you simply dreamed of being lonely, and you can't pinpoint any reason? Perhaps you need to reconnect with those around you, in case your current lifestyle is gradually making you withdrawn.

PLAYING SOLITAIRE
Are you comfortably single, but dreamed that you were walking somewhere alone and feeling isolated and miserable? If so, there is no need to worry about your emotional state, but it is worth considering the thought that you should keep your mind open to meeting someone. Perhaps you have been hurt in the past, but it's time to open up again.

NEGATIVE EMOTIONS

Related themes:
Conflict
Insecurity
Powerlessness

FEAR

If you awoke terrified by a nightmare in which you were overcome by panic, horror, or fear, what terrified you? Were you in an airplane that was spiraling downward, out of control, and are you afraid of flying in waking life? If so, such a dream may simply be a reflection of your phobia. And as appalling as the dream may have been, your unconscious mind's intention was not to torture you, but rather to encourage you to confront (and thus eventually conquer) your fear. The causes of fear dreams are not always obvious, however. Did you feel dread while you were with a friend? And if so, is there something about him or her that you fear at an unconscious level?

WAKE-UP CALL
If you dreamed that you were being pursued by someone who was threatening you with violence, can you remember who the perpetrator was? If he was a stranger, could he represent someone who does pose an actual threat to you, whether of violence or otherwise? Or, could it be that you were both the stranger and the victim? This may mean that you fear something within yourself.

MIND & BODY

Related themes:
Conflict
Jealousy
The shadow archetype

NEGATIVE EMOTIONS

HATRED

People we meet at work or elsewhere will sometimes provoke feelings of hostility in us during waking life. If you saw your dishonest colleague being hurt in your dream, yet you stood by feeling nothing but hatred, your unconscious may have been allowing you to express your antipathy in the safe haven of dreamland. But, if someone of the same sex as you switched your dream self into hostile mode through his or her offensive behavior, consider whether that person could have been your archetypal shadow. What about him or her so repelled you? Should you acknowledge this consciously suppressed aspect of yourself that you hate so much and come to terms with it?

FRIEND OR FOE?
Did you have a serious falling out with your best friend in your dream, and did you end up loathing each other? If so, this could be the result of your own guilty conscience. Does your friend know of something you've done that you are ashamed of? Or do you feel genuinely angry with him or her in real life? If so, perhaps you should avoid him or her for a while.

NEGATIVE EMOTIONS

Related themes:
Betrayal
Insecurity
Abandonment

JEALOUSY

If you dreamed that you were jealous of someone, the message is usually straightforward: something about that person makes you feel inadequate. If you can identify what it is, heed the message from your unconscious that you need to come to terms with your feelings of deficiency. If you are envious of her appearance, or his charm, for instance, ask yourself if this is a quality that you should be nurturing in yourself. Or, try to detoxify your feelings by accepting that you possess other strengths and virtues that more than make up for your self-perceived failing. If, however, someone was jealous of you in your dream, he or she has probably let slip somehow that he harbors hostile feelings toward you.

THE GREEN-EYED MONSTER

If you are in what you believe to be a secure relationship, but you saw your partner paying the wrong kind of attention to someone else in your dream, your unconscious is reflecting your feelings of insecurity. If you envy the other person, ask yourself if he or she really does pose a threat to your relationship: more likely, you need to work on your self-esteem.

NEGATIVE EMOTIONS

Related themes:
Betrayal
Shame
The trickster or shadow

GUILT

In your dream, did you succumb to temptation, only to feel overwhelmed by feelings of guilt? Did you respond to the sexual charms of an irresistible stranger, ignoring your real-life partner? Dreams like this reflect profound unconscious desires that the conscious mind has tried to suppress. If they repeatedly recur, it would be advisable to acknowledge the problem area — for example, sexual frustration — and then to try to work on resolving it in waking life. Or, did you dream that you snubbed your helpful neighbor, or that you stole from your own child? If so, maybe your conscience is troubling you about something else you've done.

REMEMBERED CRIMES

In your dream, did you relive something that you did as a child that got you into trouble, and that you still feel guilty about? Children can be miserable when they fall from grace with a parent, even though the transgression may not have been an especially serious one. If you dreamed that you were mortified by breaking something, for example, can you draw a parallel with a similar real-life event in your memory?

NEGATIVE EMOTIONS

Related themes:
Sex
Guilt
Anxiety

SHAME

Some of us repeatedly experience dreams in which we feel a terrible sense of shame, and that unpleasant feeling lingers when we awake. For example, we might be flooded with humiliation after being exposed in a dream as a fraud or as someone who has concealed a crucial character flaw. Such dreams may be among the long-term consequences of abuse suffered in childhood, when the vulnerable party—the child—is made to feel that he or she is partly responsible for the abuse. Because abusers make their victims keep quiet about their experiences, the sense of shame engendered in the victims is only deepened. If this describes your own situation, you should seek help to find peace of mind.

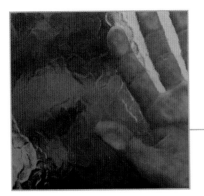

"HOW COULD YOU?"
In your dream, did you feel ashamed of yourself but, on awakening, could not work out what your supposed crime or misdemeanor was? Such dreams are usually a sign of a guilty conscience, even if your real-life guilty secret did not feature in the dream. If nothing occurs to you as the cause of your dream, could it be something you buried years ago?

Related themes:
Catharsis
Self-control
Regret

NEGATIVE EMOTIONS

ANGER

While we all suffer from angry feelings in waking life, we learn our own strategies for dealing with them and keeping them under control until they dissipate. In dreams, however, we have the luxury of letting off steam in ways that would be wholly unacceptable, perhaps even dangerous, in real life. A dream in which you saw red and reacted with unbridled fury to someone or something may, therefore, have had a safety-valve purpose—allowing you to give vent to your anger in the secure environment of the dream world. Or perhaps your dreaming mind was warning you that you are close to the edge and that your suppressed rage is becoming so overwhelming that you may soon lose control in waking life.

ROAD RAGE

Did you suffer from road rage in your dream and, instead of keeping yourself calm behind the wheel, did you berate the person who annoyed you? The key to this dream may be the identity of the person at whom you shouted. Are you angry with him in real life? Or could it have been some reckless part of yourself?

NEGATIVE EMOTIONS

Related themes:
Anxiety
Powerlessness
Loss of control

FRUSTRATION

Little is more frustrating than a machine malfunctioning. If, in your dream, your computer crashed, you were probably just as furious as your waking self feels when faced with such a setback. Are you failing to keep your computer in order, or perhaps working against a deadline with no time for delays, so that the dream is what you fear could happen? Or could the computer represent an aspect of yourself that is in danger of going wrong. Are you close to "crashing" yourself? Or, in your dream, did you miss your flight because you were frustatingly delayed en route to the airport? If so, have you missed out on a real-life opportunity?

OPPORTUNITIES MISSED

In your dream, did you almost achieve an ambition—for example, winning in your favorite sport against your main rival—but fail to capitalize on your chances, and find yourself bitterly disappointed and frustrated? If you feel that your dream near miss represents something you genuinely want, but that you have squandered your chances of achieving, try to accept it and move on.

THE BODY

Related themes:
Support
Progress
Standing up

LEGS, HIPS & KNEES

If your dreaming mind focused on your legs or knees, could there have been a symbolic meaning? For example, did you feel "weak at the knees" or that your "legs turned to jelly"? Unless they mirror an actual physical problem or waking concern, dreams of the legs, hips, and knees generally refer to issues of progress or support (or the lack of either) in the real world. So if, for example, you were limping through dreamland, or had lost the use of your legs altogether, could your unconscious have been saying that something is hampering your career progress during office hours, or come to a complete standstill? Or are you having difficulty "standing up for yourself" in a real-life setting?

MODEL THIGHS
If you dreamed that you were showing off perfect, smooth, cellulite-free thighs, how can you relate this to your present appearance? Did you once have lovely legs, but recently noticed how they had changed, and not for the better? Or are you anticipating a night out wearing your new mini-skirt, and do you have concerns for your confidence?

THE BODY

Related themes:
"Best foot forward"
"Itchy feet"
Grounding

FEET & TOES

If you dreamed that you were walking barefoot in the park, could your unconscious have been highlighting the need to "ground" yourself better in waking life? Or, if you were barefoot on the beach, do you yearn for a vacation, or more freedom? Or maybe your dream was confirming that you are at last standing on "your own two feet" now that your career has taken off, or you've conquered your thorny debt problems. Did you "put your best foot forward" as you stepped out along your dream road, or did you "drag your feet," showing reluctance? Could your dreaming self's itchy feet have highlighted a desire to travel and see the world?

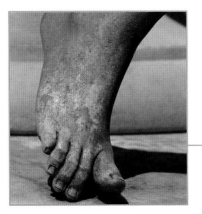

ON YOUR TOES

A dream of being "on your toes" may have signified your readiness to deal with whatever comes your way. But if your dream toes were dirty or blistered, could this be a simple message from your unconscious that you are neglecting yourself? Or were you dipping a toe in the water, checking to see whether you might try out something new?

THE BODY

Related themes:
Welcome
Embracing
Strength

ARMS & ELBOWS

In dreams, arms are often symbols of strength or weakness, and elbows may denote effort ("elbow grease") or fending something off. Arms can also signify embracing and welcoming, or else the reverse, depending upon the body language. Did your long-lost friend greet you with "open arms"? Or did your furious mother stand before you with arms akimbo? Or, did she lovingly wrap her arms around you and reassure you that everything would work out? If so, did your unconscious mind prompt you to work on a reconciliation with her in real life? In order to interpret the meaning, try to remember your accompanying dream feelings.

ELBOW ROOM

If your dream focused on an image of an elbow, several interpretations may apply. The primary one is of confidently marking out personal space by holding out the elbows from the body. If you were using your elbows to make an assertive, but not aggressive, gesture, could you have been pointing out to someone that you need some breathing space and don't want to feel so smothered?

THE BODY

Related themes:
Handling situations
Lending a hand
Hand signals

HANDS & FINGERS

Dreams involving the hands might be an indicator of your proficiency in a certain area (being "handy," for example, or being able to "handle yourself"). Did your boss tell you that he considered you his "right-hand man," or did he shake hands with you, but with a limp wrist? Did you notice your friend's clenched fists in your dream, and have you argued, or could your unconscious have been alerting you to her "tight-fistedness?" Could your dream of dropping a hot plate have been warning that you'll get your "fingers burned" if you attempt to grasp the opportunity that you've been offered in the real world, because it's "too hot to handle"?

SIGN LANGUAGE
If you dreamed that someone gestured to you with their fingers, was the meaning of the gesture clear to you? If you were shocked because you were "given the finger" by your close friend, there could be a parallel in your recent shabby treatment of him or her, or else you have picked up on a cooling off between you. On the other hand, was the gesture a "come hither" by someone you know?

THE BODY

Related themes:
Self-image
Strength
Virility and youth

HAIR

The unconscious mind often uses hair to denote intellectual and physical power and, for men, virility. Because it is also crucial to our image, the unconscious may focus your dreaming attention on your hair to reflect how attractive you are feeling. Did you dream that you'd suddenly grown a luxuriant head of hair? If so, could mirror your waking satisfaction at looking and feeling good, or else compensate for your dissatisfaction with your waking appearance. But if you struggled to run a comb through your hopelessly tangled tresses in your dream, are you wrestling with "knotty" problems, or are you trying to extricate yourself from an emotional "entanglement"?

A NEW IMAGE

If you were having a haircut in your dream, were you controlling the change to your image, or was a stylist doing it for you? Were you trying to update your look? Or was your hair proving impossible, flyaway or out of control? If you are anticipating a date with someone you've had your eye on, a dream haircut may remind you to arrange a real one, to boost your self-confidence.

THE BODY

Related themes:
Intellect
Wisdom
Reasoning

HEAD & NECK

The symbolism of the head is that of thinking, intelligence, reasoning and control. If you had a nightmare in which someone was threatening to cut off your head, who was that person? If it was your boss, is he putting you under so much pressure that you're on the verge of "losing your head"? Or, if your friend hit you over the head in your dream, are you finding her behavior a "headache"? When interpreting any dream that focuses on a head, be it your own or someone else's, consider whether your unconscious may have been referring to "getting ahead," or achieving progress, or, more simply, to your or another person's intellect (or lack of it).

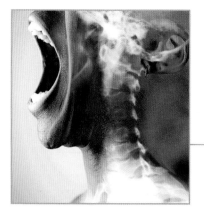

PAIN IN THE NECK

You may have felt an ache in your neck while you were dreaming, and then woken to find that you had a cricked neck, in which case your dream was caused by your actual discomfort. Otherwise, are you "getting it in the neck" from someone in waking life? Are you "sticking your neck out" over something, or even "risking your neck"? Or are you "up to your neck" in problems?

THE BODY

Related themes:
Change
Growth and ageing
Interaction

MOUTH & TEETH

Did you watch your girlfriend's lips working overtime in your dream while she berated you over something? If so, your unconscious could have been reflecting your intolerance of her constant nagging. Or, because lips are also associated with female genitalia, your dream may have been signaling a quite different reaction to her, one that only you can interpret. Most of us have the occasional anxiety dream about our teeth falling out, and sometimes the explanation has a direct connection with a real-life situation. You may have been suffering from toothache, for example. But if you are at a critical stage of life, involving a significant change, your dream may have been reflecting your emotional reaction to this.

TOOTH FAIRY
When we lose our milk teeth, we are starting to leave childhood behind. Teeth are associated with periods of momentous change in life. If you had a dream in which you lost your front teeth or were awaiting the tooth fairy, are you feeling worried about moving on, for example? Or are you concerned about losing your youthful good looks, or simply youth?

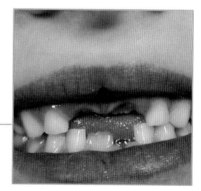

THE BODY

Related themes:
Truth
Trust
Communication

EYES

Were you facing your mother in dreamland, and did she tell you to "Look me in the eye, and tell me it isn't true"? If so, and you were unable to meet her eye, you are probably feeling guilty about having done something that you know she'd disapprove of. Said to be the "windows to the soul," eyes are instruments of unconscious communication, as well as of vision. If you dreamed that you had gone blind, your unconscious may have been alerting you to your tendency to "close your eyes," or "turn a blind eye," to the truth about something. Perhaps there is an intrigue going on under your nose that you'd prefer to ignore, rather than confront?

EYE SURGERY

If you were concerned about the bags under your eyes in your dream, or your increasingly deep "crow's feet" lines, and were considering surgery to rejuvenate your face, ask yourself whether this dream expressed your anxiety over ageing or something compromising your vision. Perhaps your unconscious is prompting you to look more clearly at what is going on around you.

THE BODY

Related themes:
Interfering
Breathing
Smelling, or perceiving intuitively

NOSES

If your dream featured a nose, whose was it, and could your unconscious have been signaling that he or she is "nosy" in waking life, spying on you intrusively or trying to interfere with your affairs? Or perhaps you looked into the mirror and saw that your normally straight nose had been transformed into a broken one. Could the break have been inflicted, in dreamland, by someone with whom you are about to fall out in the real world? If you had a blocked nose in your dream, you may have simply have wrapped yourself so tightly in your bedclothes that you were having difficulty breathing properly.

PROMINENT PROBOSCIS

Because your nose is your most prominent facial feature, if you dreamed about it, you may have been expressing anxiety about the face you show to the world. Did you have a seething boil, and were you trying to hide? Can you draw a waking parallel? Or, if you dreamed that you went out with something on your nose, you probably felt foolish when you discovered that you were the last to know.

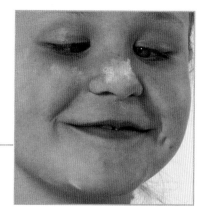

THE BODY

Related themes:
Secrets
Gossip
Communication

EARS

Hearing is as important a sense as sight for our ability to perceive what is going on around us, and then interpret our perceptions as information. Did your dreaming vision home in on an ear, be it yours or someone else's? If it was someone else's ear, was the person apparently trying to listen in on you, or find out something that you've been trying to keep secret, or else something that you wish you hadn't said about him or her? Or, was he or she trying to turn a deaf ear, or ignore you? If you had earache in your dream, it may have been a message from your subconscious that you've had enough of being nagged, bullied by your boss, gossiped about, or shouted at by someone close to you.

TUNING IN

In your dream, were you straining to hear something? Or, were you listening carefully to a conversation, but unable to make sense of it because you could not understand the language or accent? These dreams indicate that you may be feeling left out of something that you want to be part of. Are you being excluded from decisions at work?

THE BODY

Related themes:
Carrying burdens
Strength (physical or emotional)
Turning your back, or letting someone down

BACKS

If you felt that you were suffering from a backache in your dream, it may be that it was real, but if this was not so, ask yourself whether your unconscious could have been focusing on your "backbone" for a specific reason. Are you, for instance, considering backing down over a contentious family issue, and could the message have been that your intentions are "spineless"? Or is something going on behind your back? But if your spouse, for instance, turned around and walked away from your dreaming self, do you fear that he or she is about to "turn his back on you" in the waking world? If so, it may be time to resolve your recent row.

RELAXATION TIME
In your dream, if you were receiving a welcome back massage, the most likely explanation is that you have been working too hard lately, whether physically or emotionally, and you need some rest, relaxation, and perhaps some form of therapy. If, on the other hand, you were giving a massage, this may have been an expression of your concern or affection for the person you were soothing.

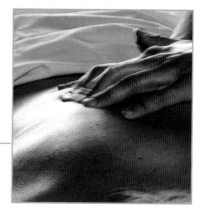

THE BODY

Related themes:
Fear of death
Vulnerability
Feeling exposed

BONES

Skeletons, skulls, and bones are all symbols of death, so if you were frightened by their appearance in your dream, this could point to your fear of dying, or of a loved one's demise. But if you were in a forest in your dream and came across a pile of bones that had been picked clean by a vulture, this may point to getting to the "bare bones," or the heart of something, when extraneous matters have been stripped away. Alternatively, this dream could signify cleansing, purifying, being reborn, or moving on. If you dreamed that you had broken an arm or a leg, consider the significance of that particular limb or body part.

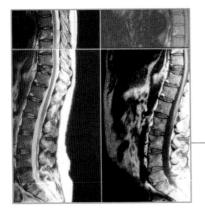

X-RAYS

X-rays and scans reveal hidden truths, so if you were worried about someone, perhaps your friend, seeing an X-ray of your head or a scan of your brain, are you concerned that he will discover the truth about you, see you as you really are, or find out what you actually think of him? Or were you poring over an X-ray with your doctor, and if so, are you anxious about your health or well-being?

MIND & BODY

THE BODY

Related themes:
Life force
Energy
Menstrual cycles

BLOOD AND BLEEDING

The primary symbolism of blood in dreamland is that of the life force. Whether you dreamed of cutting your finger while chopping vegetables or that you were more seriously injured in a knife attack, your dream loss of blood may have denoted your loss of vitality in waking life—be it self-inflicted because you've been working so hard, or because a conflict with someone is sapping your strength. Alternatively, if you are a woman of childbearing age, a dream that features blood may sometimes herald the onset of menstruation or changes in your menstrual patterns, or else reflect pregnancy-related fears or hopes.

BLOOD TEST

If you dreamed that a sinister doctor was taking your blood without your consent, did you recognize the dream doctor? If it was someone you know, the dream's significance is likely to relate to something in your relationship with that person in waking life. If, however, the dream doctor was a stranger, it may be that you are worried about losing control over your health or emotional strength.

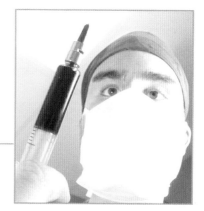

PHYSICAL FUNCTIONS

Related themes:
Emotional well-being
Anxiety
Ageing

SICKNESS AND HEALTH

Unless you are actually in the grip of a disease or illness, a dream of being sick rarely refers to your physical health, but rather to your emotional well-being. It may be, however, that by depicting you lying on your sickbed, your unconscious was warning that this is how you may end up if you don't take better care of your health. Dreams of sickness usually refer to a psychological or emotional disturbance, and your unconscious will sometimes use the language of the medical textbooks to signal where the problem lies. So try to make a link between your dream ailment and your waking life.

GOING DOWNHILL

Did you dream that you were at an important work meeting when you felt yourself unable to concentrate because you were feeling increasingly unwell? If so, is your job actually making you sick in real life, because of the stress you are under or the hours you put in? Or could the dream have reflected your confidence and your fears that you can't keep up with other, "fitter" colleagues?

PHYSICAL FUNCTIONS

Related themes:
Happiness
Mirth
Humiliation

LAUGHING

In your laughter dream, were you laughing with abandon and feeling on top of the world, or was someone else laughing at you mercilessly and making you feel small? Alternatively, were you laughing out loud while feeling far from amused, and if so, were you trying to put a brave face on something? If you were the subject of others' derision, the dream is likely to have referred to your low self-esteem and you may well have awoken feeling isolated. Try to remember who was making fun of you and whether it was over an issue you would like to change in real life, or else simply a reflection of the perpetrator's cruel streak.

GSOH

If you and your new friend or lover were sharing a hilarious joke in your dream, you were probably feeling a sense of closeness and intimacy from your shared point of view, which may have been a simple reflection of your actual relationship. But if you were unable to stop your uncontrollable laughter, could this be a sign that you aren't taking him or her seriously enough?

PHYSICAL FUNCTIONS

Related themes:
Irritation
Discomfort
Disturbance

ITCHING & SCRATCHING

If your skin was itching unbearably in your dream, you came out in a rash, or were plagued by sores, and you have discounted any physical cause for your nocturnal discomfort, ask yourself what could be acting as an irritant or allergen, or what you may be feeling "sore" about during your waking hours. Or was a particular item of clothing or type of fabric making you itch? If so, can you relate it to something that is spoiling your comfort in your waking surroundings—for example, could a tight, itchy collar reflect a constricting relationship or work situation? If you dreamed of scratching your insect bites, something is niggling you.

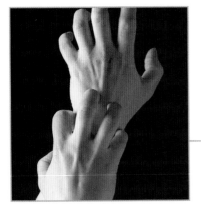

IRRITATION

If your fingers were constantly raking your skin in your dream, you were probably being driven mad by something, so can you remember what was disturbing you? Were you bitten by blood-sucking mosquitoes, and if so, what, in the real world, has been pestering you lately? Or could you simply be easily distracted from your current priority of finding a calm space in which to relax?

MIND & BODY

Related themes:
Cold
Hostility
Irritants

PHYSICAL FUNCTIONS

SNEEZING

Sneezing is usually caused by a cold or other virus, or by an allergen, or another invasive irritant to the lining of the nose, such as dust or pepper. If your dream focused on you feeling chilled to the bone and sneezing, this could mirror your hurt feelings that someone close to you has begun to treat you coldly. On the other hand, sneezing because you were in a dusty dream environment is likely to indicate that you were investigating a deserted place. Were you in a forgotten attic searching through possessions you hadn't disturbed for many years? If so, the things in the attic may have been a metaphor for memories that have been locked away.

HAY FEVER

If your dream disappeared in a virtual fog of sneezing and snuffling because you had hay fever, you may well have been suffering in your sleep and the symptoms entered your dreamlife. But if you haven't suffered from hay fever since you were a child, has something prompted you to remember summer days from your childhood? Did you recently hear from, or think about, your estranged father, for instance?

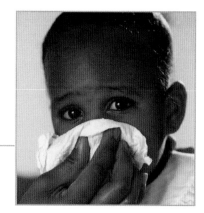

PHYSICAL FUNCTIONS

Related themes:
Purging
Indigestion
Catharsis

VOMITING & TOILET HABITS

When we urinate or defecate, we are ridding ourselves of bodily waste, and when the dreaming mind portrays us performing these functions, the reference is similar—albeit to emotional waste, such as unpleasant memories, or tough lessons you have digested that are now redundant (but are nevertheless burdening your mind). So if your dream depicted you rushing to the bathroom and emerging with relief, what would you benefit from flushing out of your system in the real world? Dreams that involve vomiting may have similar meanings, too. In your dream, did you need to "purge" yourself of a toxic emotion?

THE SMALLEST ROOM

If you were in a bathroom in your dream, were you pampering yourself, or were you sick, or were you straining to purge yourself but unable to produce a result? Since your bathroom dream was likely to have an emotional parallel in your waking life, try to find the link based on your dreaming emotional state. If you really did need to use the bathroom, however, that explains the dream!

PHYSICAL FUNCTIONS

Related themes:
Love
Self-esteem
Intimacy

SEX & KISSING

Sexual dreams are extremely common and are perfectly natural, even if your dream was of sexual behavior that you would find shocking in your waking life. The most likely explanations of a vivid sexual dream are either related to your recent sexual inactivity—and thus your sexual frustration, which you may have completely repressed for some time—or else, conversely, to your recent sexual activity. Have you just become involved with someone new, and if so, did you relive your passionate encounters in dreamland? If you had a nightmare in which you were sexually assaulted, this probably referred to a humiliating experience in the real world, or else some form of exploitation.

PLAYING AWAY

When we are in committed, settled relationships, dreaming of being unfaithful can feel like a guilty secret. If, however, you have been single for a while, a sexual dream is most likely to be a form of wish fulfillment, especially if the other player in your dream was either a stranger or someone you've had your eye on in real life.

CLOTHING
ACCESSORIES

CLOTHING & ACCESSORIES

Clothes project an image, whether consciously manipulated or accidental, which is why they are such an important part of the persona that each of us presents to those around us. As well as informing others about our personality, job, status, and values, our clothing also reflects our self-esteem, or lack of it. And when the unconscious assumes the function of a costume director in a dream, its selection of garments will tell you much about how you perceive both yourself and the people in your life. This chapter explores the dream-world symbolism associated with various types of clothing and accessories.

Related themes:
Protection
Warmth
Concealment

CLOTHING

COATS

Coats, cloaks, and overalls generally serve a practical purpose, namely to protect the wearer from the cold, or else from the dirt and debris of their working environment. So if you dreamed that you were wearing any of these garments, what sort of contamination are you trying to ward off in the waking world?

Because they can also conceal you, perhaps a dream of wearing an inconspicuous jacket is an indication that you're trying to hide the real you from others by blending into your surroundings. What is it that you are trying to cover up from the scrutiny of those around you?

WRAPPING UP

Did you dream that you reached into your closet and pulled on a heavy coat, even though it was stifling hot, before sitting down to a romantic candlelit dinner with your partner? Perhaps your unconscious was alerting you to the fact that you are involved in a cold or "icy" relationship or situation in the real world, for which you need a double layer of protection.

CLOTHING

Related themes:
Femininity
Formal occasions
Elegance

DRESSES & SKIRTS

A dream in which you were frolicking in a long, flowing skirt could indicate feelings of freedom, or else reflect a need to "let loose" in the waking world. Or, if your dress was exceptionally desirable or expensive, could it be that you long to live a life of luxury? These items of clothing are traditionally associated with femininity, so if you are a man who found your dream self happily sporting a skirt, might you be more content in the real world if you softened your approach to others? Any dream of wearing a skirt or dress in an inappropriate situation may indicate a feeling of frustration at being restricted in the real world, perhaps because of your gender.

BRIDAL WEAR
If you are a woman, and dreamed that you were wearing a beautiful wedding gown, did you feel yourself to be very pretty and elegant? This could be a reflection of your real-life feelings of happiness and confidence in your femininity. Or perhaps your dream is reflecting a more general longing to form a relationship with someone special.

CLOTHING &
ACCESSORIES

Related themes:
Mobility
Progress
Independence

CLOTHING

FOOTWEAR

Feet are a means of mobility, and dream shoes can often symbolize some sort of advancement in the real world. If you dreamed that you laced up a new pair of hiking boots and set off on an adventure, your unconscious may have been encouraging you to indulge your passion for exploration. But did your dream shoes cause you agonizing pain? Perhaps you feel that your freedom is being restricted in the waking world. Or, if you were wearing another person's shoes, could your unconscious have been advising you not to judge so quickly?

Socks that are full of holes may hint at feelings of demoralization, feelings that you may be managing to hide from others by concealing them with metaphorical shoes.

BEST FOOT FORWARD
Wearing shoes suited to a particular occasion, or inappropriate to your situation, could be an indication of whether you were comfortable in your dream scenario. If you paused, en route to work, to trade your chic heels for a pair of novelty sandals, is your unconscious mind sending you an important message about your real-life priorities?

CLOTHING

Related themes:
Celebrations
Rites of passage
Being constrained

FORMAL DRESS

Formal clothing is usually indicative of either celebratory or somber events, and so, in the world of dreams, the donning of such can symbolize a "marked" occasion; a recent engagement, perhaps, or graduation. But, because the very fabrics of formal dress denote high quality (and the means to afford them), their inclusion in dreams may also reflect a longing to be perceived as a cut above the rest. Or could it be that your dream was merely a reflection of your real-life self-esteem? If, however, you were "suffocating" in your fancy attire, perhaps you are feeling restricted by your formal duties or by the need to keep up appearances in real life, and are longing to let loose and to relax.

ALL DRESSED UP
If, in your dream, you relished the admiration of everyone around you, do you wish to present a more elegant image of yourself to others in the waking world? It could also be that you have been desiring a night out, or that you wish that you had more wealth, excitement, or leisure time in your life.

CLOTHING &
ACCESSORIES

CLOTHING

Related themes:
Relaxation
Embarrassment
The archetypal persona

SHABBY DRESS

Old or ill-fitting clothing can indicate a relaxed attitude, so if you are usually a careful dresser, but you found yourself comfortably lounging around dreamland in tatty old sweatpants, perhaps your subconscious was giving you a break from your daily, self-imposed restrictions. It may even be encouraging you to seek more rest or variety in your waking life. But if, in your dream, you were embarrassed by your ragged appearance at a dazzling party, it may be that this is a precise reflection of your waking world. Have you lately been feeling ashamed of the image that you have been presenting to others?

A STITCH IN TIME

If you found yourself sewing a patch in your dream, was your unconscious speaking in puns? Is there something in your life that needs "patching up"? If it was positioned on the sleeve of a dream shirt, perhaps, after many years of exposure, you are trying to hide something about yourself from others, such as the big, easily broken heart that you've tended to wear on your sleeve until now?

CLOTHING

NIGHTWEAR

The meaning of nightwear in dreams depends on the type depicted and the situation in which it is worn. If you dreamed that you were lounging around the house in broad daylight in a comfy nightgown, your unconscious may merely have been encouraging you to relax and catch up on some much-needed sleep. Or was your dream self humiliated when you realized that you had accidentally gone to work in pajamas? Perhaps you are feeling anxious over the sharing of private information among your real-life coworkers. Perhaps, too, if you have lately been complacent about your career, this was your unconscious mind sending you a timely reminder.

SEDUCTIVE SILK

Did you have a dream in which you enjoyed parading your body before someone while you were dressed in sexy lingerie? If so, who was the person for whom you were showing off? Is it possible that you have real-life feelings of attraction for this person? If your baiting behavior achieved the desired effect, you probably experienced a wish-fulfillment dream.

CLOTHING & ACCESSORIES

Related themes:
Work and career
Formality
Choking and strangulation

CLOTHING

SHIRTS & TIES

Shirts and ties are worn almost exclusively by professional men, so if, in your dream, you felt the irrepressible urge to loosen your collar, your unconscious may have been expressing waking feelings of restriction, maybe in relation to your job. Or did your dream find you clinging on to someone's shirttails, and are you overdependent on his help in the real world? If you rolled up your shirtsleeves, is a forthcoming task looming large in your conscious mind? Or are you in danger of "losing the shirt off your back" and going bankrupt? Don't forget, a dream shirt may simply have been an unconscious reminder of your growing ironing pile!

TIES THAT BIND

Bright shirts or neckties offer sober-suited men a way of expressing their personality (some analysts believe the tie can also be a phallic symbol). If your dreaming attention was drawn to such an item, who was the person wearing it and what did it look like? Was it flashy, conservative, colorful, or wacky, and what does its appearance say about its wearer—perhaps you?

CLOTHING

Related themes:
Vacations
Fitness
Body image

SWIMWEAR

The meaning of any dream in which someone finds themselves baring large amounts of skin will depend greatly upon the body image of the dreamer. If you were frolicking on a dream beach, unabashed in a bikini, you may well be satisfied with your appearance in real life. Or maybe you were simply enjoying a wish-fulfillment dream and it's high time that you took a vacation. But if you felt exposed, are you concerned that something personal about you is about to be revealed to the world? Or were you aghast at how badly your bikini fitted you? If so, it is likely that your dream was a metaphor for your actual dissatisfaction with your current image or body shape.

MATERNAL EMBRACE

Bathing suits, beaches, and swimming all have strong associations with summertime and leisure. Therefore, if you had a dream of being carefree in a swimsuit, you should consider whether it might have been an unconscious expression of nostalgia, particularly for your childhood (since summertime is a time of freedom for most children).

CLOTHING & ACCESSORIES

Related themes:
Sexual attraction
Infidelity
Humiliation

CLOTHING

UNDERWEAR

Worn next to the skin and beneath our clothing, underwear is highly personal and could, in dreamland, represent the more secretive aspects of ourselves. Did you enjoy flaunting your body in your dream, in front of a person to whom you're attracted to in the real world, and did they reciprocate? In dreams your wishes can come true. Or were you mortified by your near nakedness, or by stained or dirty lingerie? You could be harboring feelings of sexual guilt. And if you are a man who felt shame or panic while a crowd jeered at your undressed state, could your subconscious have been expressing concerns about your sexual potency or the exposure of your sexuality?

DRESS TO IMPRESS

In your dream, did you find yourself selecting and then dressing in a sexy thong or brightly colored bra with feelings of glee or self-satisfaction? Your unconscious may simply have been expressing your sexually playful side. If, in real life, you would choose to wear more conservative items next to your skin, could you secretly long to be more sexually confident?

CLOTHING

Related themes:
Anonymity
Conforming
Authority

UNIFORMS

The collective authority of soldiers and policemen as upholders of the rule of state and law of the land is symbolized by the depersonalizing uniform that they wear, so a dream in which a uniformed figure appeared may hint at repressed feelings of guilt about having deviated from, or infringed, a social code. It could, alternatively, highlight your desire to assert your individuality and nonconformist nature. All uniforms, to some extent, are emblems of self-discipline and the work ethic, so if, in your dream, you were the only one wearing civilian clothes, your unconscious may have been underlining your uneasiness at having fallen "out of line" with those around you.

GUIDING HANDS

Did you dream that you were lost in an unfamiliar place until a friendly officer came to your rescue? If so, do you feel that you are in need of help from some higher authority in the real world? Or if you yourself were the uniformed figure, and were pleased at the respect it lent you, could this signify an unconscious desire to change the way you present yourself?

CLOTHING & ACCESSORIES

ACCESSORIES

Related themes:
Vision
Clarity of focus
Outlook

EYEWEAR

Dreams that focus our attention on eyewear can vary greatly in their meaning. If you had a dream in which you were frustrated to find that you could not see clearly, so that you had to put on a pair of spectacles, then this could be an unconscious cue that you are being shortsighted with regard to some issue in your waking life. Or, if you donned a pair of sunglasses in your dream, have you been thinking of a vacation recently? What color were the lenses? Did your dream indicate that you have been viewing the world "through rose-colored glasses"—something that we say that people do to see the brighter side of things.

STUDIOUS TYPES

Did you have a dream in which you wore a pair of spectacles, and in which the people around you were impressed by your clever witticisms? This type of dream is an example of an unconscious play on the old stereotype that people who wear glasses are somehow more intelligent than those who don't. Have you been feeling especially wise in your waking life, or do you wish you were?

ACCESSORIES

Related themes:
The archetypal persona
Concealing something
Deception

DISGUISES

A mask is the symbol of the persona, the face that we present
to the world. If you were wearing one in your dream, what is
it about your true nature that you're concealing from those
around you? Perhaps all your dream figures were masked. If
so, could your unconscious have been referring to a real-life
situation that is also a "masquerade"? If you found yourself at
a fancy-dress party in dreamland, did your choice of costume
highlight any particular unconscious desires? If you were out-
fitted as a member of the opposite sex, perhaps that is a sign for
you to draw out your masculine or feminine qualities in real
life. It is worth remembering that fans hide the holder's face, as
do veils (which also have connotations with grief or mystery),
and hoods can have sinister associations with death.

FALSE FACE
*Did you dream that you encountered a
masked figure? If so, did you try to
snatch off the mask to reveal the person's identity? Your dreaming reaction
could have been sending a powerful
message that you believe someone to be
wearing a "false face." Who, in the real
world, do you wish would "unmask"?*

ACCESSORIES

Related themes:
Barriers
Protection
Intimacy

GLOVES

If you had a dream in which gloves were featured, the meaning will depend as much on the type of gloves that were worn as the context in which they were seen. If you saw protective rubber gloves, for example, were you consulting a doctor or undergoing dental surgery, or might someone be trying to avoid contact with you? If, in your dream, you took off your right-hand glove in order to shake hands with someone, your dream gesture reveals friendly, or at least civil, feelings for that person. But if you did not greet that person's appearance with pleasure, were you "taking the gloves off," showing your willingness to "fight dirty," whether or not the dream gloves were boxing gloves? If you put on a pair of gloves in your dream, could it have been because you are worried about "revealing your hand"?

SECOND SKIN

As gloves form a barrier between your skin and whatever you are handling, is there an unpleasant task that you'll soon have to undertake in the real world, perhaps one with which you do not wish to "dirty your hands"?

ACCESSORIES

Related themes:
Authority
Spirituality
Identity

HATS

Hats can be worn either casually, perhaps in the form of a baseball cap, or formally, as part of, say, a wedding outfit, so a dream hat could denote a laid-back attitude, a team allegiance, or, alternatively, a celebration. Certain forms of headgear denote authority. If you wore a magnificent crown, do you feel you deserve the acclaim of others in waking life? Or was someone in your dream wearing a skull cap? What does it tell you about that individual, whether or not you know him to be pious? Did you tip your dream hat to anyone, out of respect? Or was it knocked off by someone, perhaps because they accused you of having ideas above your station?

HEAD TRIP

The traditional symbolism of the head is that of intelligence and higher consciousness. A dream hat may therefore symbolize personal aspirations. If you pulled on a protective piece of headgear in your dream, are you sheltering your deepest desires from an emotional rainstorm, perhaps, or is your attention simply being focused upon this area of your life?

CLOTHING &
ACCESSORIES

ACCESSORIES

Related themes:
Identity
Style
Sexuality

PURSES, BAGS & BRIEFCASES

Handbags and briefcases are highly personal items, in which we carry everyday and emergency objects, not to mention address books and cell phones—keys to communication with the people in our lives. The loss of a dream bag or a briefcase—and, more importantly, its contents—may thus reflect anxiety about a loss of identity, or of the various aspects of our character or life that together make us unique individuals.

If, however, you were rooting around in another person's bag in your dream, you're probably curious to know more about them, to discover what makes them tick.

WHAT'S YOUR BAG?

Handbags can be symbolic of female sex organs and the womb. So if you had a dream that focused a spotlight on a newly purchased, gorgeous handbag, you should consider whether your dream was a metaphor for your real-life feelings with regard to your sex appeal. Was your dream a reflection of your waking feelings of satisfaction with your sexuality? Or could it be that you desire to appear more sexually attractive to others?

ACCESSORIES

Related themes:
Moral values
Eternity
Treasure

JEWELRY

Unless you dreamed of a specific piece of jewelry that you
either covet or actually own, dream jewelry, gems, and precious metals rarely represent themselves. Instead, these
items embody a precious abstract value or quality, such as
the inner beauty, vivacity, or purity of the recipient, or the
commitment, loyalty, love, or friendship of the giver. Rings,
in particular, symbolize unity and partnership, and bangles
and bracelets also denote wholeness and eternity through
their circular shape. In presenting you with a glittering love
token in your dream, your unconscious may therefore simply have been fulfilling—however briefly—your deep desire
to feel loved and appreciated.

STRUNG OUT?

Did you dream that a string of pearls,
that your partner had given you suddenly broke while you were fingering it?
If so, is there a weak link in your relationship, one that could cause your commitment to each other to disintegrate
completely unless steps are taken to
strengthen it?

ACCESSORIES

Related themes:
Burdens
Emotional baggage
Transition

LUGGAGE

Other than simply denoting travel, the most obvious interpretation for dream luggage is that it is emotional "baggage."
Did you have a dream in which you exhilarated in traveling light? If so, have you found the strength to cast off the
problems that you had been carrying around with you? Or
if you struggled along with heavy suitcases, perhaps you
feel "weighted down" by your real-world responsibilities.
Alternatively, if you dreamed that your suitcase broke open,
spilling all of your clothing and personal items onto the
sidewalk, do you fear that your private emotions are in danger of "spilling out" for all to see?

JOURNEY'S END
Do you wish that you could leave your old
life behind? Do you long to take a new
direction? If, in your dream, you were at
the station, bag in hand, did you know
where you were headed, or did you relish
the thrill of going off into "the great
unknown"? Did you arrive at your destination? If so, it may be that you have
already achieved your waking goal, or
that you can see yourself doing so.

ACCESSORIES

Related themes:
Identity
Femininity
Financial worries

WALLETS

Wallets are the means by which we carry those items that identify us as individuals. So if you had a dream in which you were searching through someone else's wallet, could it be that you would like to find out more about this person? Or if you lost your own wallet, did your dream reflect real-life feelings of anxiety about loss of identity or purpose?

A purse symbolizes femininity, so if, in your dream, someone snatched yours, do you feel sexually threatened in the waking world? Or, if you are a woman who dreamed that you closed your purse to keep your partner from taking money out of it, are you angrily holding back from him in the real world?

WATCH YOUR WALLET

If you dreamed that you lost your wallet or purse, did your nightmare simply reflect your general anxiety with regard to losing your possessions—perhaps because you view yourself as absent-minded or irresponsible? If this is the case, your unconscious mind may have been telling you that you must learn to be more careful with your things.

CLOTHING & ACCESSORIES

ACCESSORIES

Related themes:
Stress
Mortality
Ageing

WATCHES

If your dream focused on a timepiece, it is important to consider the context and your dreaming reaction to it. It may have been measuring the passing of your lifetime! If you dreamed, for example, that the hands of your clock moved unbearably slowly, could this have reflected your sense that time is dragging, maybe because your waking hours are so boring? Are you eagerly anticipating the arrival of an important day? Or could the dream clock symbolize your heart, or "ticker," thereby highlighting a cardiac problem (of which you may already be aware)? Alternatively, if time passed too speedily in your dream, making you late, this may be an unconscious reference to missed opportunities, impeded progress, fatigue, or stress.

STOP THE CLOCK
Did you dream that you were running late for an important business meeting, but, instead of speeding up in distress, you slowed your pace and calmly turned into a coffee shop for a slap-up breakfast? A dream like this may have been an unconscious plea to slow down and to make some more time for yourself in the waking world.

ACCESSORIES

Related themes:
Protection
Emotional "storms"
Being prepared

UMBRELLAS

The umbrella is a symbol of protection (and rain shares water's symbolic association with the emotions), so if, in a dream, you were required to use one, you should ask yourself whether you are being besieged by a storm of emotions in real life. Did a dream friend shelter you under their umbrella, or were you the one who protected someone else? If your umbrella was broken or blown away by a big gust of wind, did you dump it in the trash and march on without it (perhaps to find that the rain wasn't so bad, after all)? Or were you caught out in the rain without any protection at all? If so, your unconscious may be warning you that you need to think ahead in order to protect yourself because there are "rainy days" ahead.

STAYING DRY

In your dream, how well did your umbrella shield you from the rain? The answer could be a clue to how well you are protecting yourself from the emotional battering that you have been undergoing in real life. Did your umbrella leak? If so, perhaps you need to find a new means of defense from whatever is besieging you.

ACCESSORIES

Related themes:
Change
Moods
The archetypal persona

STYLE AND IMAGE

Did you astonish yourself in a dream of shopping for clothes, when you excitedly picked out a garment that you'd never consider wearing at all in real life? If you normally dress conservatively, for instance, and you dreamed of wearing a daring new style, your unconscious may have been indicating that you have become too set in your ways. Or was such a dream reflecting your own yearning to break out of a rut and to catch the attention of a certain someone? Conversely, if you dress casually during your waking hours and you dreamed of wearing a suit, could your unconscious have been hinting that you should be projecting a more professional image?

COLOR-CODED

Were you surprised by the color of clothing that you wore in your dream? If so, does that hue have personal significance to you, so that you respond to it either positively or negatively? Your own associations apart, bright colors express cheerfulness, while dark shades convey sadness. White denotes innocence, and black, mourning.

FOOD & DRINK

When we eat and drink in the real world, we are usually responding to the triggers of hunger and thirst. But unless you went to bed hungry, or became dehydrated during the night, dreams that feature food and drink rarely refer to a physical requirement for nourishment, instead pointing to a need for emotional, intellectual, or spiritual sustenance, or else sensory, or sexual, gratification. Dreams of being thirsty or getting drunk; of cooking, comfort eating, enjoying a meal, dieting, or gorging on food; or of particular foodstuffs, therefore, all send powerful messages about your current state of mind.

FOOD

Related themes:
Growth
Birth
Potential

EGGS

The symbolism surrounding eggs is ancient and profound. It focuses on birth (either literal or metaphorical), spiritual regeneration, and growth. If you are a woman who is hoping to have a baby in waking life, a dream of an egg may, therefore, have reflected your desire to conceive. But if you were gathering eggs from a dream chicken coop, yet you decided to leave one behind, could your dream have been highlighting the potential "hatching" of an idea that is currently gestating in your mind? If you discovered a golden egg, can you relate this treasure to something you are either seeking or have recently found in real life?

BAKER'S DOZEN

If you dreamed of a basket of eggs, are you actually contemplating putting "all of your eggs in one basket" by taking an all-or-nothing gamble in the real world? Or, consider the possibility that the number of eggs had some significance— for example, did you count to thirteen, and are you superstitious? If, however, your eggs were cracked, this may point to damage to your plans or a project.

FOOD

Related themes:
Fertility
Temptation
Sustenance

FRUITS & VEGETABLES

Fruits have long been associated with both immortality and feminine fertility. The latter is particularly true of rounded, soft fruits, while some long, rigid fruits and vegetables, like bananas and cucumbers, are phallic symbols. So, your dream of fruits or vegetables may have had an erotic dimension. Fruits are also associated with temptation, and because they are sweet, with rewards and success (as in the phrase "coming to fruition"). Vegetables provide vitamins and other nourishment necessary to our health and well-being, so their appearance in a dream is likely to signify emotional sustenance, if not nourishment of the body.

MARKET DAY

If you were shopping for food in your dream and stood before a display of vegetables, what was your dream reaction? If you have always resented being forced to eat vegetables by your parents, and now live on processed foods and take-out meals, could your unconscious mind have been suggesting that you confront your dietary habits and make some sensible improvements to your lifestyle?

FOOD

Related themes:
Survival
Substance
Wealth

BREAD & MEAT

Bread has been a staple food for centuries in the West, which is why its primary symbolism is that of life and survival. If, in your dream, you had nothing to eat but a stale hunk of bread, the implication is that you are facing poverty or need. This could refer to the lack of either financial means or spiritual or emotional sustenance. Do you fear going hungry in the literal sense, or can you relate this to your feared or actual emotional poverty? Meat has overlapping symbolism as a staple food, but has other meanings, too. Something that is "meaty" is rich, tangible, or filling. Your dream of a meat-laden table implies feasting and wealth rather than poverty.

DINNER IS SERVED

Did you dream that you were being served a delicious rack of lamb, and are you an impoverished student, subsisting on a simple diet made up of inexpensive staples like rice and potatoes? If so, your unconscious mind may have simply reflected your desire for a more satisfying dinner, perhaps like those you once took for granted in your family home. But if you are vegetarian, is someone ignoring your opinions and preferences?

FOOD

Related themes:
Rewards
Achievements
Ease or difficulty

SUGAR & DESSERTS

If you dreamed of savoring the sweet sensation of eating honey, sugary cookies, pies, cakes, or desserts in your dream, your unconscious may either have been expressing satisfaction with the sweetness of your actual circumstances at present, or else compensating you for their bitterness. Is your life currently as "easy as pie," or do you wish that it was? Are you longing for a "piece of the cake," or are you already enjoying it? But if you dreamed of eating sugary popcorn, is an element of childish fun and excitement lacking from your waking world? Or, are you dieting, and if so, was this a wish-fulfillment dream?

CANDY CANES

When, in your dream, you drooled over candy canes, cotton candy, or a similar childish delight, were you allowed to eat the treats, or could you only look on enviously while someone else ate them? This dream could be a reflection of your real-life diet, in which you are denying yourself sweet, sugary foods. But if you are not on a diet, do you long to return to the relative simple days of your youth?

FOOD

Related themes:
Practical support
Preparations
Nurturing

COOKING

If you were the cook in your dream, dishing up dinner for your family, it is likely that your family members rely on you to give them love, comfort, and support. So did you feel contented or resentful as you prepared the dream meal? And because a cook transforms raw, often indigestible, ingredients into a palatable dish, is there something that you're "cooking up" during your waking hours, perhaps a plan that's simmering in your mind that you hope will soon be ready to set before others? Similarly, if you were baking, what could you have been incubating in your dream oven?

BAKING DAY

If your dream was a return to childhood and someone else was bustling around the kitchen in an apron, was it your mother? If it wasn't your mother, and you were cooking with someone else, you probably regard him or her as a source of emotional sustenance. On the other hand, it could be that you are embarking on a project with the other person, and you are yet to find out how well you will work together in the real world.

FEASTING & FASTING

FOOD & DRINK

Related themes:
Emotional deprivation
Comfort eating
Ambition

HUNGER

Dreams of being hungry are often related to emotional, as opposed to physical, sustenance. Were you so ravenous in your dream that you went rushing urgently up and down the street looking for a fast-food restaurant, but in vain? If you later awoke feeling equally starving, your dream was almost certainly literal. Otherwise, the explanation for your dream appetite may lie elsewhere. Deprivation sharpens the appetite, so ask yourself for what you are hungering during your waking hours. Could it be the comfort of a fulfilling emotional or sexual relationship, or the satisfaction that comes from enjoying your job and doing it well?

RAVENOUS!

Dreams relating to the appetite may be set in our remembered childhood, when we were nervous of trying unknown foods and comforted by our favorite dishes. In your dream, if you felt overwhelmed by hunger, but then tucked into a burger—then your most prized treat—did all suddenly feel right with the world? Comfort food in dreams, as in life, can help us through unhappy times.

FOOD & DRINK

FOOD & DRINK

FEASTING & FASTING

Related themes:
Nostalgia
Family
Anxiety and conflict

FAMILY GATHERINGS & HOLIDAYS

Many of our holiday celebrations center around a family meal, as do special birthdays and anniversaries, and the dining table becomes the place where our families get together to relax and share the celebration. If you dreamed of a happy holiday gathering, like those of your childhood days, your unconscious might have been reminding you of happier, more carefree times when you were unaware of adult pressures and problems. But if you are the person responsible for serving up a large, festive dinner, and you are busy and stressed, or else if you are part of a new, uneasy stepfamily or have relatives who don't get along, dreaming of a holiday feast could be an anxiety nightmare.

BIRTHDAY CAKE

If you dreamed that you were a child again, blowing out the candles on your birthday cake while your family looked on indulgently, are you now single and living far from your family, without a supportive network of people to make a fuss of you? Birthdays and holidays are often the focus of our dreams when we are lonely or adjusting to change.

FEASTING & FASTING

Related themes:
Hunger
Dieting
Indulgence

OVEREATING

Like dreams of being hungry, dreaming that you are over-eating may signal a lack of something in your life. Did you dream that you had ballooned into an obese person, and were you so shocked by your bloated appearance that you immediately resolved to go on a fast? This dream may mirror your waking anxiety, even obsession, about eating and your weight, in which case, you should probably be seeking help for your problem. Or maybe you were bingeing greedily on a mountain of food in your dream even though you weren't hungry. If this was the case, could you be indulging in something for the sake of it—perhaps reading or watching movies all the time instead of facing up to your problems?

MORE, PLEASE!

In most cultures, turning down someone's hospitality is considered rude or, at the very least, inconsiderate. So if you are a vegetarian who dreamed that you were invited to Sunday dinner at your in-laws' house, did you try to compensate for your avoiding the chicken by eating as much of everything else as you could? If so, maybe you feel the need to live up to their expectations of you.

FOOD & DRINK

Related themes:
Self-denial
Guilt
Self-control

FEASTING & FASTING

DIETING

If your dream focused on the need to diet in order to lose weight, do you feel weighed down by weighty problems that you long to shed in the waking world? Otherwise, could your dream have implied that you are suffering the consequences of overindulging, not necessarily in food, but perhaps in a hobby with which you've become obsessed, so much so that your waking life has become unhealthily imbalanced? If your dream was concerned with being too thin, however, have you been starved of vital nourishment—be it emotional, sexual, or intellectual—in the real world?

ON THE SCALES

If you climbed on the scales in your dream and worried over your weight, are you counting calories in your waking hours at the moment? If not, it is likely that your dream was related to either self-control or self-denial. You may have pressing money worries, for example, and your daily concern over what you can afford to spend has manifested itself as the need to be careful about what you are eating.

DRINK

Related themes:
Relaxation
Stimulation
Mornings

COFFEE & TEA

Did you enjoy a cup of tea or coffee and a good gossip with your best friend in dreamland? Coffee and tea are consumed when people are in need of a break, or, in the case of coffee, when the brain needs a kick start. Do you feel the need for more relaxation or stimulation? Dreaming of drinking with friends at a coffee bar may refer to a social life that has dwindled into nothing and could do with reviving. Coffee is associated with morning routines, so if you dreamed that you left the house without your morning cup of coffee, perhaps you are undergoing or contemplating a change of routine.

BEAN SCENE

Drinking coffee at a stylish venue has become a way of "seeing and being seen," so if you were at a dream coffee bar, were you waiting to meet someone? If you had arranged to meet a blind date, were you feeling confident about yourself, or were you looking down at your cup, nervously stirring your coffee? On the other hand, if you've been feeling good about yourself lately, your dream might have reflected your easygoing life.

DRINK

Related themes:
Celebration
Loss of control
Partying

ALCOHOL

Alcohol equates to fun and relaxation for some people, and to loss of control to others. If you felt suffused with a sense of well-being as you shared a beer or a bottle of wine with someone during your dream, your unconscious may have been showing that you'd benefit from enjoying some stimulating conversation while you relax in the company of friends in the waking world. And if you popped open a bottle of champagne in your dream, are you celebrating a real-life achievement, or are you hoping to? If, however, you were lurching drunkenly all over the place, are you in danger of losing emotional control in real life?

JUST ONE MORE

In your bar dream, were you reluctant to continue drinking because you felt guiltily aware that you were becoming inebriated, yet you were unable to resist the drinks that were put in front of you by your companion or the bartender? This dream indicates that you are being manipulated or led into temptation by someone, or else you feel that you lack the willpower to stick to your limits.

DRINK

Related themes:
Mother
Childhood
Security

MILK

Maybe you dreamed that you made yourself a mug of warm milk and observed to your dreaming self that this reminded you of your childhood, when your mother used to give you a drink of milk at bedtime. If this is the case, and you are finding waking life particularly demanding, your dreaming mind may have provided you with a sensation of warmth, comfort, and security, such as you enjoyed when you were small, in compensation for your currently stressful circumstances. But if you held a hungry baby and could not find any milk, what is making you feel inadequate in real life?

MILK AND COOKIES

Because we relied on our mothers for milk when we were babies, your dream of looking contentedly at a glass of milk may have been referring to your need to be mothered and cherished by a maternal figure (if not your actual mother). If problems have been piling up around you, or you are under too much pressure, in your waking life, this dream may have been a reflection of your need to forget your responsibilities.

FOOD & DRINK

DRINK

Related themes:
Life
Emotions
Refreshment

WATER

Did you dream that you were besieged by an overwhelming thirst for a long drink of cool, refreshing water as you were making your way through an arid, sun-scorched landscape? If so, you may simply have become hotter and thirstier as you slept, and your unconscious worked your physical discomfort into your dream. If you don't believe that this explanation applies, however, considering your dream in symbolic terms may enlighten you. In the language of the unconscious, water is often used as a metaphor for the emotions, so could it be that you are beginning to feel emotionally parched, perhaps because you have been single for so long in waking life?

WATER OF LIFE
In symbolic terms, water is linked with femininity, the unconscious mind, and the emotions. So if you were drinking deeply from a water bottle or fountain, did you feel rejuvenated and refreshed? This dream could signify that you have found something that is emotionally important for you, such as a rewarding relationship or a sense of peace.

ACTIVITIES & ACTIONS

If you dreamed of your favorite pastime in dreamland, your unconscious may simply have been reflecting your conscious preoccupation with your hobby. But if your dream depicted you engaged in a leisure occupation that plays no part in your waking hours, was your unconscious passing comment on your current approach to life? And when trying to interpret the meaning of any dream in which you received or sent a message, consider whether the communication made a clear reference to something about your waking life and think about what you associate with the dream messenger. Remember, too, that dreams that focus on negative actions are rarely predictive.

ACTIVITIES & ACTIONS

Related themes:
Progress
Ambition
Competition

MOTION

RUNNING

Running is associated with moving forward in waking life. Its significance in dreams has little to do with physical advancement, however, instead reflecting how well you are doing in your quest to achieve your ambitions. This is why it's helpful to take careful note of a number of aspects of your dream when attempting to analyze it. What exactly were you running toward? Were you tired or did you run effortlessly? Were you competing against the clock or rivals? Were there any obstacles in your path? Did you reach your destination? The answers to these questions about your dream will help you to assess your progress and to identify anything that stands in your way.

ON THE RUN

Did you dream that you were in pursuit of another person? If so, is this someone whom you've been "chasing," or seeking to make a connection with, in the waking world? Has this person been drawing away from you emotionally of late? Alternatively, if you were running in order to escape someone or something, ask yourself what it is in real life that is making you feel threatened.

MOTION

Related themes:
Hurdles
Decisions
Change

JUMPING

In real life, we jump from one position to another either to clear a hurdle in our path or to get from A to B more swiftly. If you found yourself jumping in your dream, your unconscious mind was probably drawing a parallel with some aspect of your waking life. By depicting your dreaming self executing a perfect jump, for instance, your unconscious may be signaling that you have made, or are considering making, a quantum leap, perhaps in the form of a significant decision. If, however, you stumbled and fell, your dream may be warning you that you have either made the wrong choice or are in danger of doing so.

A LEAP FORWARD

Do you know why you were jumping in your dream, or what it was that you were jumping to reach? Were you making a "leap in the dark," into unknown territory, or were you simply "jumping for joy," and, if this is the case, is there something in your waking life that is a cause for celebration? In your dream, did you miss your target, stumble, and fall?

ACTIVITIES & ACTIONS

Related themes:
Water
Beaches
Docks and Harbors

MOTION

SWIMMING

Unless you feel that your dream was simply highlighting a need to relax, or reflecting a real-life phobia, dreams of swimming usually hint at your current emotional state, or else a need to listen to your unconscious mind. If you dreamed of diving into the sea, were you penetrating the depths of your unconscious in search of insight? If you were swimming smoothly through calm waters, this indicates that your conscious and unconscious minds are working together in productive harmony, but if you dreamed of struggling against a strong current, are you battling a powerful urge in the waking world? And if you were out of your depth in a dream ocean, are you feeling emotionally helpless in real life?

FLOATING

Did you dream that you were floating blissfully, not thinking of anything at all as you relished the sensation of the warm water caressing and supporting your apparently weightless body? If your waking hours are fraught with anxiety, your unconscious may have been trying to comfort you by returning you to the security of the metaphorical womb.

MOTION

Related themes:
Partnership
Conforming
Self-expression

DANCING

If you dreamed that you were dancing in dreamland, were you dancing alone, with a partner, or with others? If you were gracefully ballroom dancing with another, your dream may have been highlighting someone who is actually, or who you long to be, your partner in real life, be it your spouse, business partner, or best friend. So did your dream mirror your sense of being "in step" with that person? Perhaps you dreamed that you were dancing in a group. If so, your unconscious may have been either reflecting your tendency to conform, or else your habit of "stepping out of line." How well did you keep time with the others in your dream?

DANCING A SOLO

A dream of dancing on your own may have been expressing your waking feelings of joyfulness. But if you had your eye on an attractive someone in the dream scene and were hoping that your sensuous moves would attract his or her admiration so that you'd soon be dancing cheek to cheek, your dream may have had erotic overtones.

ACTIVITIES & ACTIONS

MOTION

Related themes:
Promotion
Progress
Power and strength

CLIMBING

In your dream, what were you climbing? A ladder may denote the "corporate ladder" (as, indeed, may each step of a flight of stairs), or it may alternatively be a phallic symbol, with connotations of masculine power and mastery. A dream hill or mountain signifies a greater challenge, denoting the large scale of a task on which you are focused in real life. The summit signifies the apex of your personal aspirations, be they professional, social, or spiritual. Did you keep the pinnacle in your sights? Did fallen rocks obstruct your progress? Did you have a climbing companion? Examining such aspects of your dream will tell you more about the nature of your approach to achieving your goal and your chances of success.

AIMING HIGH
Did you reach the object of your ascent and feel on top of the world? If so, your dreaming mind is encouraging you by telling you that you have the ability to re-enact your achievement in that aspect of your real life in which you harbor ambitions. If your goal eluded you, however, the message may be that your aim is either unrealistic or too daunting to attain.

MOTION

Related themes:
Progress
Direction
Confidence

HIKING AND WALKING

Always consider how you were moving in a dream, and try to make a connection with your attitude to your waking life at present; the parallel will usually be clear. Did you dream that you were limping? This may have implied that your freedom of movement is somehow being restricted in the real world. Dragging your feet may have signified reluctance; strutting, arrogance; and tripping or stumbling, taking a wrong step or making a mistake. And if you were horrified to find that you couldn't move at all, your unconscious may have graphically depicted your sense of having come to an abrupt standstill in the waking world.

STROLLING ALONG

Did you dream that you strode vigorously and with confidence along a wide, straight road on a sunny day? If so, the incidental symbols incorporated into your dream bode well for the future. The sunshine, for example, suggests a sense of optimism and well-being, while your straightforward route implies that you know where you are headed in life.

ACTIVITIES & ACTIONS

Related themes:
Discovery
Seeking or researching something
Burying or hiding something

MOTION

DIGGING

Did you dream that you seized a shovel and started digging a hole in the earth because you hoped to uncover something, and did you then find anything? A dream like this may have a number of meanings. You may, for example, be carrying out a research project during your waking hours, but need to "unearth" a vital piece of evidence before you can complete it, in which case your dream discovery may have symbolized that crucial missing link. Otherwise, could your unconscious have been alerting you to the need to "get to the bottom of," or learn the truth about, your friend's behavior, which has been suspiciously out of character recently?

FINDING YOUR ROOTS

If you are consciously preoccupied with finding out more about your family history, was your dream of digging mirroring your quest to discover more about your "roots"? But if you dreamed of burying something in the earth, what are you trying to "bury," cover up, or hide from others in the real world? A shameful secret, perhaps, the very thought of which makes you feel "soiled," or dirty?

MOTION

GARDENING & YARD WORK

If you are a gardener, you will know that cultivating the earth can reap astounding rewards, which is why the earth is associated with the bountiful fertility of "Mother Earth," also the giver of sustenance, stability, and security. Plant a seed, and, if the conditions are right, the earth will encourage its germination, as well as providing the nourishment that it needs for growth and solid foundations in which to root itself. Could your dream of gardening have referred to an intellectual or creative seed that has recently been planted, or taken root, in your fertile imagination, one that has the potential to blossom and bear fruit if cultivated and cherished?

EARTH MATTERS
If your dream depicted you sowing a seed in the dark, rich earth, try to make the link between the dream scene and your waking world. Could the seed have represented the baby that you and your partner are hoping to conceive in real life, and the soil, the physical and emotional nurturing that it would receive, enabling it to grow and thrive in a loving and supportive family environment?

ACTIVITIES & ACTIONS

Related themes:
Health and well-being
Repetition and routine
Burdens and weights

MOTION

WORKING OUT

If you dreamed of working out, your unconscious may have simply been urging you to safeguard your health and exercise more in your waking hours. If you don't think that this explanation applies, however, could your dreaming mind have been encouraging you to build up your strength (not necessarily physical, but perhaps intellectual or emotional), or else could it have been making a link with how you are feeling in the real world? If you were running on a treadmill in the dream gym, for instance, was your unconscious implying that your waking life has become dreary and repetitive and is being marred by your sense of getting nowhere? If you were lifting weights in dreamland, could they have represented the heavy burden that you have shouldered in the waking world?

ARDUOUS REGIME

If a dream fitness instructor was yelling at you to perform fifty more reps when you were already exhausted and on the point of collapse, do you feel that you are being pushed beyond your limit, perhaps by someone who has authority over you, during your waking hours?

MOTION

Related themes:
Teamwork
Leadership
Cooperation

PLAYING TEAM SPORTS

Most dreams in which you were playing a team game reflect how effectively you are performing within a group situation in waking life. So if you dreamed of playing baseball, football, hockey, or volleyball, for instance, are you interacting in dynamic harmony with your fellows? Are you the linchpin that holds everyone together, or do you envy another person's star quality? Are you letting the side down by being lazy or clumsy, or do you blame someone else for being the weakest link that consistently undermines your team's collective efforts? Are you a "good sport," or do you cheat and throw a tantrum when things don't go your way?

HOME RUN

Did you dream that you hit a vital home run in a professional sporting contest? If you are actually a baseball player, your dream is doubtless concerned with wish fulfillment. But what might it mean if you are, in fact, a hopeless athlete? Perhaps your unconscious mind is rewarding you for having done well at something that you may not consider very significant in waking life.

ACTIVITIES & ACTIONS

Related themes:
Independence
Competition
Rivals and opponents

MOTION

PLAYING INDIVIDUAL SPORTS

If you dreamed of being an individual sports competitor, your unconscious was probably drawing a parallel with your self-sufficiency in forging your way through life. Who was your opponent in dreamland, and who was the dream victor? Whether you were running, cycling, skating, or skiing, if you were powering your own sporting progress in dreamland, and particularly if there was no one against whom to measure your success, your unconscious may otherwise have been drawing a parallel with how adeptly you are controlling your efforts to get ahead, and how smoothly and rapidly you are advancing toward your goal in waking life.

ON FORM

Did you serve an ace in your dream? Perhaps your unconscious was commending you on your outstanding performance in the real world. But if you missed shot after shot, was your unconscious warning that your current lack of application is causing your skills to become rusty? Or was your racket faulty? Could your unconscious have been advising you to update the tools of your trade in waking life?

RELAXATION

Related themes:
Cleansing
Pampering
Emotions

BATHING

If you had a dream in which you were taking a shower or bath, is there something that you are anxious to cleanse yourself of? Or, in your dream, were you frantically trying to "wash your hands of" something? Or, as in the song, is there someone that you wish that you could "wash right out of your hair"? Dreaming of any of these activities implies a need to cleanse your conscience of some problem or issue. Or perhaps you had a pleasant dream, in which you were sharing your bath with another. If so, was this other person known to you? As water can symbolize the unconscious mind, is there someone with whom you wish to share your innermost secrets?

A SOOTHING SOAK

Did you dream of luxuriating in a hot bubble bath, perhaps with soft music playing, a glass of chilled champagne in your hand, and masses of candles emitting a gentle light and heavenly scent? If so, your unconscious was probably taking the opportunity to give you a bit of the rest, renewal, and rejuvenation that you are so desperately craving during your waking hours.

ACTIVITIES & ACTIONS

RELAXATION

Related themes:
News
Knowledge and learning
Entertainment

READING

The written word can inform, enlighten, and stimulate the mind in both the real and dream worlds. In dreams, books have symbolic associations with wisdom, so it is important to remember what it was exactly that you were reading. Newspapers and magazines are also sources of knowledge, yet their contents are more ephemeral and quickly become outdated. Dreaming of reading one of these daily or weekly publications may have reflected your conscious anticipation of receiving some important news in the real world. Or perhaps you are unconsciously looking for ways of incorporating more variety and interest into your waking hours.

LETTERS

Did you receive a dream letter? Who was it from, and was there anything out of the ordinary about its script? If it appeared shaky, could your unconscious have been stressing the sender's real-life vulnerability? Were any words capitalized or underlined? Or was this communication typewritten or word-processed? Do you and the sender have an impersonal connection in real life?

RELAXATION

Related themes:
Self-expression
The blues or other emotions
Performance

SINGING

A dream of singing in a choir is similar to one of playing in an orchestra, in that your unconscious mind places you in a situation where it is imperative to play your part in close collaboration with others in order to create a harmonious atmosphere. In your dream, were you in tune and keeping time, or was the resulting sound messy and discordant, and what might this say about your real-life relationships? If you were singing solo, your unconscious may have been mirroring your feeling of being in the limelight during your waking hours. How did events unfold? Was your unconscious reflecting your anxiety about your performance in a forthcoming real-life situation, or was it boosting your confidence by fulfilling your desire to impress your audience?

FROM THE HEART

If you dreamed of unleashing your vocal talent on a rapturous crowd, you may simply have been expressing joy, or else experiencing a wish-fulfillment dream. What is it that you long for in real life: is it the luxurious lifestyle and popularity implied by celebrity status?

ACTIVITIES &
ACTIONS

RELAXATION

Related themes:
People
Relationships
Confidence

PARTYING

When your unconscious brings you together with others for a common purpose in the parallel universe of dreams, it often does so to pass comment on the nature of your interaction with those with whom you are in contact in waking life.

Did you dream of attending a party? If so, the individuals who surrounded you, your dreaming reaction to their presence, and the events that occurred during the course of your dream all send significant messages about your personal likes and dislikes, your self-perceived status within your family, social, or professional circle, your self-confidence, your insecurities, and your individuality.

LET YOUR HAIR DOWN

Whatever it is that they are celebrating, parties give people the opportunity to mingle, be it to get to know one another socially, to network, or simply to have fun in a relaxed atmosphere. So if you were giving a party in your dream, could it therefore have reflected your desire to widen your social circle, to forge new business contacts, or to let your hair down among friends?

COMMUNICATION & INTERACTION

TALKING

If a noise made by a human voice was the most striking aspect of your dream, it is vital to consider your dreaming reaction to that sound. If you dreamed that your wife was nagging you to start exercising regularly, did your unconscious put these words into her mouth to tell you the truth? Indeed, in the language of dreams, your sleeping mind's choice of words often communicates a truth of which you are unconsciously aware, but consciously prefer to disregard, which is why a dream voice can sometimes be said to be the voice of your conscience. If you heard a number of voices whispering in your dream, however, do you fear that others are gossiping about you?

TALKING THE TALK

If you were having difficulty communicating in your dream, did this mirror your self-perceived inability to connect with others in the real world? Was everyone talking in a foreign language? If so, could your dream have reflected your waking sense of being excluded from your social circle? Or was your friend speaking so quietly that you struggled to hear? Are you unreceptive to her point of view in real life?

ACTIVITIES &
ACTIONS

Related themes:
Conflict
Aggression
Distress

COMMUNICATION & INTERACTION

SCREAMING AND SHOUTING

If you dreamed that there were two or more of you shouting at one another, who were these people, and how harmonious is your relationship in waking life? It may be that your dream merely mirrored your mutual dislike. If it was you who instigated and dominated the argument, your dream may have been giving you an outlet through which to safely release your feelings. It may be, however, that the person with whom you were arguing represents an aspect of yourself—an interpretation that is even more likely if your adversary was a stranger. What did he or she look like, and can you remember what the argument was about and who accused whom of what?

CRY FOR HELP
Were you, or someone you know, screaming in dreamland? If so, your unconscious was probably confirming your own emotional torment, or the distress that the person's anguish is arousing within you during your waking hours. Or were your yells a cry for help? And who caused you to scream in your dream? Is it the same person who is terrifying or enraging you in the real world?

COMMUNICATION & INTERACTION

ACTIVITIES & ACTIONS

Related themes:
Rivalry
Hatred
Conflict

FIGHTING

In your dream, did your verbal sparring with someone escalate into a physical fight? The unconscious mind depicts such dramatic clashes to try to shock you into recognizing a simmering conflict in your life. Try to work out what your dream conflict symbolizes, and to identify what each participant represents in your waking life. Did you overpower your opponent, or were you subdued? And how did your disagreement finally end? A peaceful conclusion indicates that you may be able to settle the conflict (whether it is raging within yourself or between you and another individual). If the dream argument wasn't settled, however, that area of conflict in your life is likely to be a continuing source of problems.

BOXING CLEVER

If you dreamed of boxing, wrestling, or practicing a martial art, such as kickboxing, karate, or judo, your dream may have had unambiguously hostile or defensive undertones. Was your dream opponent someone you know? But your unconscious may alternatively have been urging you to control your aggression in a disciplined manner in real life.

ACTIVITIES &
ACTIONS

Related themes:
Conflict
Weapons
Power

COMMUNICATION & INTERACTION

WARRING

Unless you are (or were) a soldier who saw action on the field of combat, dream battles usually signify some real-life conflict, either between warring aspects of oneself, between two individuals, or else between groups of people. Could your dreaming mind be warning you that you will soon become embroiled in such a conflict? Whenever the dreaming mind highlights weaponry, it does so for one of several reasons: to underline straightforward feelings of hostility toward someone (maybe you); to warn that you may soon need to defend yourself; or (according to Freudians) either to express an unconscious urge to gain sexual mastery over someone, or to reflect a sexual insecurity. Were you wielding the weapon in your dream war, or were you being threatened? And who was your enemy?

SWORD FIGHT

Was someone swinging a mighty sword in your dream? Swords may represent spiritual protection, but they can also denote kingship, and may consequently denote the highest level of authority. Because they are double-edged weapons, however, swords can equally be negative symbols of malevolent power.

COMMUNICATION & INTERACTION

Related themes:
Endings
Control
Fighting

KILLING

Dreams of killing may point toward an internal conflict. If you strangled a stranger in your dream, did you feel provoked? If so, how? The answer may tell you what it is about yourself that you are longing to "kill off." Animals symbolize aspects of our instinctual nature, so if you casually killed a dog in your dream, ask yourself what the dog could represent within you. If someone was trying to murder you in your dream, your unconscious may have been alerting you to a real-life emotional threat. But if you are unable to identify your dream killer, your unconscious may have been symbolically communicating your sense of being victimized in waking life.

MURDER!

Did you wake with a start from a dream in which you furiously murdered a loved one in the heat of the moment? If you are angry with this person in waking life, you probably had a safety-valve dream, in which you were able to give rein to your rage in the most dramatic of ways without causing them any actual harm. Have you lately been feeling as if you are on an emotional "knife's edge" in real life?

ACTIVITIES &
ACTIONS

Related themes:
Recording
Messages
Self-expression

COMMUNICATION & INTERACTION

WRITING

An unsullied piece of paper offers an opportunity to make a fresh start, and a pen, a means with which to express your thoughts. So, do you remember whether you were about to write a letter or the opening line of a novel in your dream? If your dreaming intention was to compose a letter to your sister, from whom you regret having become estranged in the real world, your unconscious may have been prompting you to initiate contact with her in reality. But if you enjoy writing, and you secretly believe that you have a best-seller in you, was your dream encouraging you to put pen to paper and get your masterwork written?

WRITER'S BLOCK

The message implicit in writing in dream-land may have been that you feel an urge to communicate with someone in particular, or else with a wider audience. A dream of watching a cursor blinking away at the top of a blank word-processing document may have held a similar message, but if you associate computers with work, maybe the reference was to communicating with a business associate.

COMMUNICATION & INTERACTION

ACTIVITIES & ACTIONS

Related themes:
Secrets
Puzzles
Security

USING SIGNS OR CODES

If you are deaf or hard of hearing in real life, your dream of using sign language was probably a reflection of your everyday communications. If this is not the case, consider the following. In the real world, codes and signals are used either to keep sensitive information secret from outsiders or enemies, or, in the case of alternative communication systems like shorthand or Morse code, to convey information as briefly and speedily as possible. Any dream in which you sent or received a coded communication that you could decipher may, therefore, have been advocating the need for secrecy, brevity, or speed when communicating with a certain someone in waking life.

BODY LANGUAGE

If you were unable to understand a friend's signal, or if she passed you a note that was written in indecipherable code, the implication was probably that you are currently finding the workings of her mind incomprehensible. And if the action of your dream then descended into chaos because of your misunderstanding, is it perhaps time to address this real-life communication problem?

ACTIVITIES &
ACTIONS

Related themes:
Workplaces
Speed
Remote communication

COMMUNICATION & INTERACTION

EMAILING AND FAXING

Although the message inherent in a dream of an electronic communication is likely to parallel that implied by a letter in dreamland, urgency may be the crucial difference, as emails and faxes can be sent and received virtually instantaneously. But then, immediacy is not always a desirable quality. Perhaps you dreamed that you faxed a vicious message to your boss by mistake. If so, what was the message inherent in your dream? Your unconscious was probably warning you to keep your temper on a tight leash and to consciously restrain your tendency to act impulsively, because such behavior may have disastrous and widespread repercussions in waking life.

ANNOUNCEMENTS

A dream of e-mailing a memo to your coworkers announcing that you are intending to quit smoking and asking them to be supportive may have expressed your desire to "go on record," or to publicly state your intention (an action that would, of course, make it more difficult for your weak-willed self to sabotage your own efforts to kick your habit).

COMMUNICATION & INTERACTION

ACTIVITIES & ACTIONS

Related themes:
Intimacy, or lack of it
Making contact
Frustration

TELEPHONING AND TEXTING

Like emails and faxes, telephones and cell phones enable instant communication. The message of a dream in which you called someone, or answered a call from them, is almost certainly that that person is on your mind. But was the ensuing conversation one-sided? This may have confirmed your waking sense of grievance that someone actually does appear completely uninterested in you. Alternatively, was your unconscious trying to tell you to become more assertive? And, depending on the context, dreaming of making a phone call may sometimes remind us of the urgent need to set up a meeting or appointment before it's too late.

INSTANT MESSAGE

Did you dial someone's number in a dream and then became increasingly frustrated as they didn't pick up? Have you been anxiously trying to communicate an important truth about yourself during your waking hours, or did your dream reflect your real-life worries about this person's health and safety? And if you dreamed of calling the emergency services, what are you afraid of in real life?

ACTIVITIES & ACTIONS

Related themes:
Control
Direction
Power

GETTING AROUND

BIKING

Dream vehicles can tell us whether we are in or out of control in our waking lives. When we jump onto a bike and pedal off down the road in waking life, for instance, we are powering and controlling our own movement, although we have to put more personal effort into getting ahead than if we were walking. A bicycle does, however, enable us to cover greater distances, and if you dreamed of coasting rapidly along a smooth surface, having built up so much momentum that you hardly had to touch the pedals, the implication may have been that, thanks to your previous endeavors, you are currently advancing speedily and easily through this phase of your waking life.

SCRAMBLING

If you are male, a dream of mounting and riding a motorbike may have been commenting on your sex drive. Did you feel comfortable on your bike, or did you have difficulty controlling it? The former scenario suggests that your conscious mind and sexual urges are working together harmoniously, while the latter may have expressed your sexual inhibitions or your sense of being at the mercy of your libido.

GETTING AROUND

Related themes:
Emotions
Water
Docks and harbors

SAILING

Water-going vessels like boats and ships have similar symbolic significances in dreams to airplanes, although, because they transport us over water, their meaning is usually concerned with the realm of the unconscious, with emotions and instincts. So if you dreamed that you were sailing the high seas as a passenger on an ocean liner, was your dream advising you to embark on a voyage of emotional self-discovery, to "anchor" yourself in a loving relationship, or to actually book the cruise that you've long been meaning to take in the waking world?

PLAIN SAILING

If you dreamed of being in the middle of a sea crossing, your unconscious may have been commenting on the ease (or otherwise) of your current progress in life. Are you doing well in the waking world? Do you feel that this phase of your existence is "plain sailing" (in other words, proceeding smoothly)? Are you being buffeted by stormy weather (be it spiritual, intellectual, or emotional)? Or are you "lost at sea," or beset by uncertainty and confusion?

Related themes:
Transition
Anonymity
Surrendering control

GETTING
AROUND

TRAVELING ON A BUS

Did you dream of getting on a bus, finding a seat, and then gazing out of the window at the passing scenery as your journey commenced? The significance of such dreams lies in both the implied surrender of our ability to control our individual freedom of movement and the identity of our fellow passengers. In the real world, most buses are owned by a corporate entity, which employs drivers to steer its vehicles to their destination, as well as conductors to ensure that passengers abide by company rules. If you recognized any of your coworkers in your dream, or, indeed, if you knew that you were traveling to work, was your unconscious referring to your career path?

LIFE COACH
Could your dream bus have represented the organization for which you work; the driver, your manager; the conductor, your supervisor; and the other passengers, your fellow employees? If so, were you content to sit quietly on the bus, or did you argue with the conductor (thereby acting out your real-life resentment of the authority of your bosses), or even try to disembark (implying that you wish to leave your job)?

GETTING AROUND

TRAVELING IN A CAR

Some analysts assert that a car is a symbol of masculine sexual energies, but remember, when interpreting your dream, that it may simply have represented freedom and independence, or even (if it was not your real-life vehicle) wish fulfillment. Alternatively, a dream automobile's appearance can symbolize your persona, the steering wheel your conscious mind, and the engine and gas that fuels it your inner power. If you feel this to be so, did your dream depict you driving smoothly, or did your trip go wrong, and, if so, can you draw a parallel with your real-life situation? If you dreamed of speeding, are you driving yourself at too fast a pace during your waking hours?

IN THE DRIVING SEAT

If you were driving someone else in your dream car, it is likely that you feel responsible for steering him or her in the right direction in life. But if someone else was at the controls, could the implication have been that this person is "taking you for a ride," or else that you depend on that individual to make decisions for you in real life? Were you happy to cede control, or was this occurring against your will?

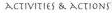

ACTIVITIES & ACTIONS

Related themes:
Speed
Spirituality
Vacations or business travel

GETTING AROUND

FLYING

In the real world, airplanes enable us to transcend the delays and difficulties of land-based travel by transporting us swiftly through the air and then depositing us at our destination. And because air can symbolize spiritual or cerebral aspirations, and the freedom within which to achieve them, if you dreamed of taking to the skies in an airplane, there are three interpretations to consider. Firstly, could your unconscious have been encouraging you to explore your spirituality or to rise above the limitations of daily life in order to concentrate on "higher" issues? Secondly, did it depict you on the fast track to a spectacularly successful career? Or, thirdly, was it advocating jetting off to an exotic location to enjoy a much-needed vacation?

FLYING HIGH

Dreaming of piloting an airplane and of performing aerial acrobatics in a clear sky is often a sign of confidence and success. If you were enjoying the exhilaration and freedom of swooping through the air in your dream, while surveying panoramic views of the landscape below, you are probably in control of your destiny and quite comfortable with your waking life.

GETTING AROUND

TRAVELING ON A TRAIN OR SUBWAY

Trains travel on tracks, so if you dreamed of being a rail passenger, could the implication have been that you are unable to deviate from the course that others—maybe authority figures in your life, such as your parents—have set for you? Did your dream indicate that you are "on the straight and narrow," "on track," "on the right lines," or being carried along the correct route to your destiny? Or did it warn that your life is in danger of "derailing," or becoming dysfunctional? Also note that Freudians associate trains with virility, so if you dreamed of being on a train that had broken down at the entrance to a tunnel, might this have been commenting on your less than satisfactory sex life in the waking world?

GOING UNDERGROUND

Dream tunnels may symbolize points of transition, while the depths of the earth may symbolize your unconscious, so if you had a dream in which you were traveling by subway, might this have signified your journey into your own unconscious in order to find the key to your potential transformation?

ACTIVITIES & ACTIONS

Related themes:
Service
Car travel
Control

GETTING AROUND

TRAVELING BY TAXI

Did you dream of hailing, and then getting into, a taxi? If so, was the driver of the dream taxi one of your friends? Taxis usually offer a quick and direct means to our destination in real life, albeit at a price, and it follows that your intended goal, and especially the person who charged you your fare in your dream, may have had relevance to your waking situation. It may be, for example, that you are hoping to switch jobs in the real world, and that your friend is in a position to put in a good word for you with her company. She may be offering you a shortcut to a new venture in life, but your dream may have been warning that she will require reimbursement (but not necessarily monetary payment) in return for the favor.

SITTING BACK

If you dreamed of being stuck in a taxi while you were taken miles and miles out of your way, who was the driver? Might your unconscious have been hinting that you are being controlled or manipulated by someone in your waking life? Is this person leading you astray and pulling you away from what might be a more suitable path in life?

ANXIETY DREAMS

Dreams of being engulfed by feelings of anxiety are among the most common of experiences in the dream world. To a greater or lesser extent, we are all plagued by such dreams, particularly at times of stress in our waking lives. This stress can play itself out in all manner of ways, perhaps most familiarly in dreams of falling or of being pursued. Whether or not we can consciously identify the cause, these dreams all stem from deep-rooted worries about our self-perceived inadequacies or external threats to our emotional security in our waking life. Whenever you have a dream like this, try to pinpoint exactly what it was that caused you the most anxiety.

ANXIETY DREAMS

THREATS & PROBLEMS

Related themes:
Claustrophobia
Being stifled
Restrictions

BREATHING DIFFICULTIES

Did you wake up from a dream in which the atmosphere was stifling and airless? If so, it may simply have been that your bedsheets were obstructing your nose or mouth while you were sleeping. If no physical cause is likely to have accounted for your dream, however, could your unconscious have inflicted the symptoms of suffocation on your sleeping self to force you to recognize how you are feeling when you're awake? Whatever you decide caused you to fight for air in your dream, your unconscious was probably warning you to broaden your horizons, free your mind, and let some metaphorical "fresh air" into your waking life.

BREATH OF FRESH AIR
Did you dream of donning a gas mask in order to escape some dangerous fumes? In real life, do you feel suppressed and are you longing for a solution? Perhaps you are in an unsatisfactory relationship and feel that your lack of freedom is stifling your individuality. Or do you feel that your dead-end job is killing your intellectual creativity? Are you searching for "inspiration" in the waking world?

THREATS & PROBLEMS

Related themes:
Burdens
Depression
Powerlessness

BEING BURIED ALIVE

In your dream, did your efforts to climb out of a hole dislodge the earth above you, so that you were pinned to the ground? Did you lie in the oppressive darkness, fighting to breathe and desperately trying to claw your way out? Why did your sleeping self dream up this horrific scenario? The most probable explanation is that you have allowed the demands, obligations, and worries of daily life to get so on top of you that you have become paralyzed with depression and feel that you are at the bottom of a "black hole" from which you can see no way out. If this is so, consider seeking the help of a professional counselor.

IT'S A COVER-UP
Was your dreaming self certain that someone (maybe a real-life work rival) deliberately buried you alive? By depicting you in such a nightmarish position, your unconscious was almost certainly trying to force you to consciously recognize that person's overwhelming hostility toward you, and his or her desire to see your hopes and ambitions "dead and buried."

ANXIETY DREAMS

Related themes:
Being trapped
Frustration
Self-denial

THREATS & PROBLEMS

BEING IMPRISONED OR RESTRAINED

Did you dream that you were locked up or immobilized by ropes or chains? Dreams of being imprisoned or restrained usually send a signal that you are feeling frustrated because something in your life is preventing you from acting freely and from realizing your potential. Did you see your captor in your dream? If so, are you feeling trapped within some situation from which you feel there is no escape? In such instances, it is likely that your unconscious is highlighting your feelings of powerlessness in an attempt to urge you to break free. And if you were gagged, it is probable that you feel that someone, or something, has taken away your freedom of speech.

HOLDING BACK
Could your dream restraints represent your own inhibitions? It may be that your bonds are self-administered, in order to protect yourself from the potential emotional hurt that may result from being true to your nature. Another possible explanation is that you are nervous of making a life-changing decision, preferring instead to maintain the status quo rather than risk failure.

THREATS & PROBLEMS

ANXIETY DREAMS

Related themes:
Power
Control
Loss of freedom

KIDNAPPED

The motives for kidnapping are more concerned with preemption, possession, and the establishment of total mastery over a target or targets than causing physical hurt. Who seized you against your will in your dream? If it was your new boyfriend, have you been perturbed by the dominant tendencies that he's started to display, and are you now beset by anxieties that he is aiming to take complete control of your life and to restrict your freedom of action? Particularly if the circumstances are unspecific, dreams of ambush or abduction may be warning that you are on the verge of ceding control of your life—but to whom, or what, only you will be able to work out.

BODY SNATCHERS

In your dream, Were you snatched from your bed? Dreams of abduction may highlight worries about being forced to leave your comfortable routine or cozy circle of family and friends. If, for example, you are agonizing over whether to accept or reject an opportunity to move away from your hometown or job, your unconscious may be trying to shock you into staying.

Related themes:
Secrets
Missing out
Obstructions

THREATS & PROBLEMS

BEING LOCKED OUT

In the language of dreams, locks and keys symbolize secrets, problems or puzzles, and solutions, and any of these meanings may be implicated by a dream of being locked in or out of someplace. Dream locked doors may also be associated with secrets, as well as closed opportunities or things that are being withheld. How did you respond to your dream of being locked out? Were you curious? Frustrated? Furious? And do you know what lay beyond the door that was barred to you? The answers to these questions should tell you whether your interest has been piqued by a tantalizing secret or whether you feel that you are being denied access to an opportunity or hidden knowledge.

UNDER LOCK AND KEY
Did the locked door of your dream lead to a room? If so, what type of room? Consulting the chapter "House and Home" may give you more clues as to the meaning of your dream. It is worth noting that Freudian dream interpreters associate locks and keys with the female and male sexual organs, respectively. Might your dream have had a sexual meaning?

THREATS & PROBLEMS

ANXIETY DREAMS

Related themes:
Financial worries
Loss of independence
Emotional reserves

DEBT & MONEY PROBLEMS

If you dreamed that you were on the verge of financial disaster, your unconscious may have been reflecting your real-life worries. Alternatively, dreams of going bankrupt often refer to the potential loss of cherished nonfinancial resources or personal qualities that give you the power and confidence to move through life. If you were disturbed by such a dream, ask yourself what your lost riches could symbolize. The love of your friends and family (are you risking all that you hold dear by being sexually promiscuous)? Your integrity and self-respect (are you in danger of becoming morally bankrupt)? Your physical vigor (are your energy reserves about to be exhausted)?

DEBT OF HONOR
A dream debt may sometimes denote a "debt of honor" or a favor that you should repay to someone. To whom are you indebted, and for what? Did a neighbor recently take care of your house while you were on vacation, or has your partner been standing by you during a recent period of hardship? Such dreams often indicate feelings of guilt, so perhaps it's time to repay your "debt" in waking life.

ANXIETY DREAMS

THREATS & PROBLEMS

Related themes:
Frustration
Lack of progress
Overcoming problems

OBSTRUCTIONS

During dreams of being chased, we may be running as hard as we can, only to find ourselves despairingly facing an impasse. This is the unconscious mind's way of telling us that we have come to a "dead end," that there is no way of escaping the fears that pursue us. Equally, our flight may be hampered if we become trapped in quicksand, enter a minefield, or are burdened by carrying an ever-increasing weight on our shoulders, all of which denote being held back by forces, and perhaps dangerous ones, beyond our control.

THROUGH THICK AND THIN

Did you have a dream in which you were walking along a trail that was so disused and overgrown that you had to struggle and fight your way through the dense foliage that blocked your way? And, in your dream, was your way blocked by a large boulder or a fallen tree? Did you persist onward, clearing the foliage and scaling the tree? If you dreamed of overcoming the obstacles that blocked your way in dreamland, it is a likely sign that you are having similar success in the real world.

THREATS & PROBLEMS

ANXIETY DREAMS

Related themes:
Fear
Indecision
Powerlessness

PARALYSIS

Did you have a dream in which you found yourself rooted to the spot and powerless to move, despite the fact that you were being pursued? It may be that you are suffering from a real-life emotional paralysis in the face of a situation that requires a drastic decision. Alternatively, as may be its purpose in conjuring up a dream impasse, your unconscious may be reflecting your feelings of powerlessness and/or hopelessness regarding an apparently unsolvable problem in your waking life. Does something, or someone, make you feel as though you are wedged in between a rock and a hard place?

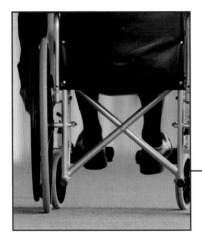

SHUTDOWN

There is a physical cause for dreams of being paralyzed. Particularly during R.E.M. sleep, the brain shuts down the body's nerve impulses to prevent us from literally acting out the screenplay of our dreams and thus endangering ourselves. Should you regain a measure of awareness during sleep paralysis (which is unusual, but does happen), your unconscious mind may then mirror your physical paralysis in your dream.

ANXIETY DREAMS

PERSONAL ISSUES

Related themes:
Guilt
Humiliation
Trust

BETRAYAL

Betrayals have been the fodder of drama and tragedy through the ages. The idea of betrayal is made much more sinister by the fact that, in order to betray someone, the betrayer must first have that person's trust—so, by definition, we may only be betrayed by a friend or a loved one. In your dream, were you outraged to find that your best friend had revealed your deepest secret to the world? Has your waking mind detected that your friend's loyalty to you may be wavering? Or was your dream a simple reflection of the growing distance that you have felt between yourself and your friend? Or are you feeling guilt over some betrayal that you have perpetrated?

CHANGING PLACES

If you dreamed that your real-life partner left you in favor of a new lover, it is almost certain that this was simply reflecting your own insecurities regarding your ability to keep his attention and prevent him from straying. That said, you may have unconsciously detected a real-life growing distance between the two of you. Perhaps its time to talk!

PERSONAL ISSUES

Related themes:
Inner torment
Competitors
Instincts

BEING CHASED

Who or what were you fleeing from in your dream? If you did not recognize the person who was chasing you, it is possible that he or she represents an aspect of yourself that you are anxious to escape, particularly if the pursuer's appearance repulsed you and if he or she was of the same sex. Could that tormentor have been your shadow? If so, what frightened you the most about him or her? Maybe the predator was a monstrous being or man-eating tiger. Again, such non-human pursuers usually symbolize an internal fear or need. They generally represent an aspect of your instinctual, nature that you may have been suppressing in waking life.

CUT TO THE CHASE

If you know the person who was chasing you, in your dream, try to work out why you may be feeling threatened in the real world. If you were being chased by someone you work with, or are acquainted with, it may be that your unconscious has detected his or her feelings of hostility toward you and is sending you a graphic warning to be on your guard.

ANXIETY DREAMS

Related themes:
Isolation
Relationship breakdowns
Misunderstandings

PERSONAL ISSUES

COMMUNICATION PROBLEMS

As in the biblical story of the Tower of Babel, when communication breaks down completely, so does the functionality of society. A dream of having difficulty in communicating may signal a real-world misunderstanding, an inability to voice your feelings or opinions, or a sense of emotional isolation. Did you have a nightmare in which you were in some sort of danger, but when you opened your mouth to cry for help, no sound would emerge? If so, do you feel unable, for whatever reason, to ask for help in the real world? Do you feel that others ignore you in the waking world, or do you have difficulties expressing how you are feeling?

CUTTING OFF

Because they enable us to bridge enormous distances and speak to people who are many miles away, telephones symbolize direct communication when they feature in dreams. Dreams of deliberately terminating a conversation with someone, by hanging up while they are talking, suggest that you similarly long to sever your connection with him or her in the waking world, even if only for a short while.

PERSONAL ISSUES

ANXIETY DREAMS

Related themes:
Breakdown
Extreme pressure
Overwhelming emotions

DROWNING

Did your dream of swimming in the ocean take a turn for the worse as you found yourself desperately trying to keep your head above the water? Unless you actually have a water phobia or have suffered a similar experience in real life, when your unconscious may have been either graphically expressing your anxiety or forcing you to relive your memories, this nightmare is likely to have signaled emotional, not physical, danger ahead. Whatever the cause in the real world, its effect has almost certainly been to unleash a storm of unconscious emotions, powerful urges, and basic instincts. Is your current situation so desperate that you are heading for a nervous breakdown?

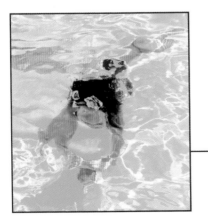

LIFEGUARDS

If you were saved, in your dream, who was responsible? It may be that you unconsciously believe that this person has the power to throw you an emotional lifeline in the real world, thereby rescuing you from the inner turmoil that is threatening to engulf you. Did you manage to save yourself? Do you hold the key that will enable you to reassert conscious control over your waking problems?

PERSONAL ISSUES

Related themes:
Insecurity
Losing face
Humiliation

EMBARRASSMENT

Embarrassment is the basis of many different types of anxiety dreams. Generally speaking, dreams of being embarrassed may signify insecurity, and a fear of appearing foolish in public or in front of someone whom the dreamer wishes to impress. Did you have a dream in which you did something that caused everyone around you to laugh and point at you? And did nobody come to your defense or aid? This sort of dream is likely to indicate that you feel insecure, and that you fear doing things that will make you appear silly or foolish in public. If so, asking yourself why you are feeling insecure will help you move toward laying your fears to rest.

JILTED

If you had a dream in which you were mortified with embarrassment because you were stood up on a hot date, or even on your own wedding day, who was the person that you were supposed to meet or marry? Do you feel a fervent desire to impress this person in the waking world, and if so, why? Do you harbor unacknowledged romantic feelings for him or her, and are you scared of rejection?

PERSONAL ISSUES

ANXIETY DREAMS

Related themes:
Lack of trust
Loss of control
Fear of failure

FALLING

Some types of falling dreams can simply be attributed to a real-life fear of heights, and some can be attributed to a muscular spasm that is known as a myoclonic jerk (a physical action that can occur during the hypnagogic state before you are fully asleep), but the falling dreams that perhaps cause us the most anxiety are those that the unconscious mind uses to draw our attention to our insecurity and fear of losing control or failing in some area of our lives. When interpreting your dream, ask yourself what you are afraid of falling from. Grace, favor, power, or the position that you have worked so hard to secure? Or is there something, perhaps a relationship, to which you are resolutely clinging because you are petrified of letting go of it?

FALL FROM GRACE

In your dream fall, did you wake up in midflight or did you reach the ground? If you did hit the ground, you were probably surprised to find little, if any, harm done. In all instances, your unconscious is trying to push you to identify a source of fear and to try to find a resolution to it, even if it means lowering your aspirations or accepting your failings.

ANXIETY DREAMS

PERSONAL ISSUES

Related themes:
Frustration
Liberation
Disempowerment

BEING INVISIBLE

Depending on the context and the mood, a dream of being invisible can either be very liberating (in that real-world invisibility could allow you to escape from problems and responsibilities), empowering (because you could presumably come and go and do as you pleased), or disempowering (probably a reflection of your real-life feeling that you are "invisible" to, or overlooked by, others). If, in your dream of being invisible, you were able to play tricks on your enemies or perform beneficient acts for yourself and your friends, your dream may have been a form of wish fulfillment, especially if you are a person with a high profile who longs for a degree of anonymity.

NOWHERE MAN

If you were horrified, in your dream, to discover that you'd become invisible, do you feel that people ignore you in the real world? Or is your waking "invisibility" self-imposed because you are unwilling, or feel unable, to allow others to see you as you truly are? If so, your unconscious may have been urging you to assert your unique personality more often so that others may get to know the "real you."

PERSONAL ISSUES

Related themes:
Stress
Being overburdened
Lost opportunities

LATENESS & DELAYS

Are you constantly juggling the conflicting demands of your high-pressure job and a growing family, and do you often find yourself running late and failing to finish tasks? You probably dream quite frequently of running late if your waking life is subject to such stress; you must find some way to take a little time for yourself to relieve the buildup of pressure that is leaking into your dreams. Such dreams may warn that you are becoming worn out, especially if you dreamed that you were too tired to summon up the energy to catch up. Or was someone else responsible for your dream delay? If so, do you blame him or her for hindering your progress in waking life?

MISSING THE BUS

Did you dream that you were running as fast as your legs could carry you, anxiously checking your watch in case you missed the bus, only to see it pull away from the bus stop ahead of you. If this is so, ask yourself if you are frustrated at having missed some opportunity in real life. Buses and trains are also public vehicles, so do you feel that others are forging ahead and leaving you behind?

PERSONAL ISSUES

Related themes:
Concentration
Cluttered mind
Losing control

LOSING SOMETHING

Did you dream that you'd lost a real-life treasured possession? If so, you may indeed have noticed during your waking hours some risk to its safety, in which case your dream could have been underlining the need to do something before you incur the loss of it in real life. Similarly, if you have actually lost something and your dream depicts you finding it again, it is worth checking the location highlighted in your dream because you may be unconsciously aware of the item's whereabouts. Such dreams sometimes also warn that you are becoming distracted and have started to lose your powers of concentration, focus, and your ability to manage the minutiae of life.

LOST AND FOUND

If you dreamed that you lost, and were searching for, something that has no immediate significance to you, your unconscious may have conjured up your dream loss as a symbol of something that is missing from your life. If you were searching for a key, for example, is a solution to a pressing problem eluding you? Or could it be the key to self-knowledge?

PERSONAL ISSUES

ANXIETY DREAMS

Related themes:
Being in a rut
Aimlessness
Loss of identity

BEING LOST

As you progressed through your dream, did you panic at the sudden realization that you'd become hopelessly lost? If so, your unconscious mind may have been highlighting your loss of direction in waking life and, by implication, the need to get back on the "right track." Ask yourself in what sense you may have "lost your way." It may be, for example, that you are confused about how best to proceed in a relationship or along a career path. Alternatively, your dreaming mind may have been warning that you have started to lose your sense of identity, your innate knowledge of exactly who you are and where you are headed in life. Identify the problem area, and then consider your options carefully, before moving forward.

NO DIRECTION HOME

In your dream, were you frightened to find yourself lost in a foreign city and too embarrassed to ask for directions? Did you then struggle with a map that you simply couldn't make any sense of? If so, your unconscious mind may have been reflecting your loss of personal focus in the waking world.

ANXIETY DREAMS

Related themes:
Loss of privacy
Shame
Vulnerability

PERSONAL ISSUES

NAKEDNESS IN PUBLIC

If you've experienced a dream of being naked in public, did you feel deeply ashamed and humiliated? Or did you rather enjoy the disapproval of the people who witnessed your nudity? Or were you the only one aware of your nakedness? The clothes that we wear are an aspect of the persona, or social mask, that we don in our dealings with others, so that, when we are naked, all artifice and pretension is stripped away, enabling others to see us as we really are, or our true selves. Your unconscious may have cast you in this situation for a variety of reasons. Are you worried that others find you ridiculous? Or do you fear that the real you is somehow flawed?

THE NAKED TRUTH

If, in your dream, you felt liberated by your nudity, your unconscious mind may be telling you that it's time to cast off your restrictions, inhibitions, and pretences, and to feel free to reveal to others who you really are. And, if you were the only one who noticed your nudity, your unconscious is probably encouraging you to "expose" yourself by indicating that no one will bat an eyelid if you do.

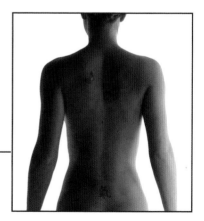

PERSONAL ISSUES

ANXIETY DREAMS

Related themes:
Insecurity
Victimization
Self-loathing

BEING RIDICULED

Whether or not they mirror reality, dreams of being ridiculed are a likely indicator of feelings of insecurity in social situations—and, particularly if these dreams are recurring, they may point to a deeply held pain, anger, and views of the self as a victim. Who was judging you in your dream? Was it someone, or more than one person, to whom you feel you need to prove your worth in real life? Can you remember what you were ridiculed for? If so, ask yourself whether your critics may have had a point. Also consider whether your merciless evaluators could have represented self-critical aspects of yourself. If so, do you either tend to judge yourself too harshly, thereby lowering your self-confidence, or, alternatively, do you consciously close your ears to your inner critics even though their comments, while admittedly hurtful, may actually be helpful?

LAUGHING STOCK

If it's been a while since you were a student, but your dream depicted your old schoolfriends pointing and laughing at you, is your unconscious reflecting your waking feelings of insecurity at your achievements since reaching adulthood?

ANXIETY DREAMS

PERSONAL ISSUES

Related themes:
Guilt
Fear of failure
Lack of confidence

BEING UNPREPARED

If you are a student who is facing an important exam in real life, did you have a stressful dream that the dread day had dawned? Perhaps you found yourself sitting at a desk feeling totally unprepared and, as you read the test paper, you panicked as you realized that you were unable to answer the questions. If so, your dream is merely expressing your fear of failing the test (although your unconscious may also be warning you that you need to study harder). The same fear-of-failure explanation applies to other types of dream tests, including driving tests, interviews, auditions, and presentations, particularly if one is pending in your waking life.

MATERNAL EMBRACE

Are you are an adult whose examination days are long past, and yet you were horrified to find yourself stuck in a dream exam hall? In this case, the test is probably a metaphor for a testing situation that you are facing in your professional life, while your dream reaction mirrors your waking lack of confidence. Have you been set a challenge at work that you feel ill equipped to meet?

HOUSE & HOME

Jung famously termed the house the "mansion of the soul," and most analysts agree that residences can be symbols of our holistic selves in our dreams. To interpret your dream, decide whether it was mostly literal or whether it relates to some aspect of yourself, and take note of the emotions that the house evoked in you. What form did your dream home take and how was it presented? The appearance of the façade may be related to your persona — how you present yourself to other people — and hence also to your feelings of self-respect. And how easy was it to gain access to the house? If it was difficult, have you erected barriers around yourself in real life?

HOUSE
& HOME

Related themes:
Persona
Memories
Emotional security

HOME

HOMES

If you dreamed of your actual home, are you currently preoccupied with some aspect of it in your waking life? Or was your dream home one from your childhood? If you were happy there, this may signal a yearning for the security or carefree times that you enjoyed at that time, or may reflect feelings of nostalgia. If, however, you dreamed of a house that you associate with unhappy memories, it may be that you are repressing feelings about something that happened there that you need to face up to in order to move on. But if your dream home was a house that you've never seen before, this suggests that you are considering making a dramatic change to your life.

INTRUDERS

Dreaming of your home being invaded sends a powerful warning: is someone trying to violate your privacy by forcing his or her way through your personal defenses? Another interpretation may be that you fear being robbed of something that you value, not necessarily your own cherished possessions, but perhaps a new idea, your integrity, or your good looks. Try to pinpoint the source of your fear.

ROOMS

Related themes:
Cleansing
Catharsis
Moving on

BATHROOMS

Bathrooms are rooms in which we clean our bodies and rid ourselves of waste matter—and in the language of dreams, it is easy to apply these functions to the emotional realm. If you dreamed of washing your hands or taking a bath or shower, is there something that you're anxious to "wash your hands of," someone that you wish you could "wash out of your hair," or troubles that you long to send spiraling down the plughole? All of these actions imply the need to cleanse yourself of an issue that is tainting your conscience, while using the toilet implies a need to relieve, or even purge, yourself of problems or unwanted feelings or memories.

MIRROR IMAGE

We all tend to look at ourselves the most critically in the bathroom mirror, under bright lights. If, in your dream, you finished washing your face and glanced up at your reflection, what did it look like? Did you see a different person? Did your appearance please or worry you? The answers to all of these questions relate to your self-image.

ROOMS

Related themes:
Refuge
Privacy
Intimacy

BEDROOMS

Like bathrooms, bedrooms may be associated with an upper story in terms of dream-house symbolism, meaning that they have to do with a level of consciousness that is a step higher than our day-to-day, "ground level" thoughts and concerns. Was your dream bedroom your ultimate personal refuge, a place where you felt safe and secure enough to surrender yourself to the oblivion of sleep? Or was it a bower of love? Your answers to these questions will usually reflect your current needs, be they for rest and recuperation or erotic stimulation and sexual satisfaction.

RESTING UP

Most people spend periods of illness and recuperation mostly in bed. So if you dreamed that you were lying in your "sickbed," or were convalescing in your dream bedroom, there are a number of possible interpretations. For example, could your dream have been an unconscious warning that you need to take better care of yourself? Or do you desire a temporary release from your real-world daily duties and responsibilities?

ROOMS

Related themes:
Social life
Emotional state
Nurturing

LIVING ROOMS, DINING ROOMS & KITCHENS

How did your dream living or dining room look? Relaxing and comfortable, elegant and imposing, cluttered and untidy, or dusty and shabby? These are the rooms in which we usually entertain guests, and their decoration and condition in your dream will tell you how you regard, and socialize with, those whom you invite into your home, that is, the collective body of people with whom you have contact in your waking life. Did you enter your dream home's kitchen? Kitchens are rooms in which we transform raw ingredients into meals and dishes with which to feed and satiate ourselves and others, thereby giving both physiological and emotional satisfaction.

FOOD FOR THOUGHT
What did your dream kitchen tell you about how well you nourish yourself or, alternatively, are nourished? Is your emotional life replete, or is it starved of love and affection? Did the kitchen encourage you to linger by offering rich food for thought, or was it a barren room that depressed you because it offered no temptations or stimuli?

HOUSE & HOME

Related themes:
Personal quests
Hidden qualities
Buried and repressed issues

ROOMS

SECRET ROOMS

In the strange world of dreams, a dream of searching or exploring your home is often symbolic of a spiritual or emotional quest—a quest to find or know your "inner" self. If you were astonished when you stumbled across a secret room while touring a dream house that you thought you knew, be it in the basement or on one of the above-ground stories, you should consider whether it represents a quality that you never knew you possessed. Now that your unconscious has prompted you to discover it, will it provide you with inspiration, along with the wherewithal and self-confidence to take a new direction in your waking life?

CLUTTER COLLECTION

In your dream, was your secret room a not-so-inviting place? Was it, in fact, a place that filled you with anxiety, fear, or apprehension? Did you spring open the door to discover a terribly dirty and messy room that was packed high and full of old junk and garbage that you thought you'd gotten rid of years ago? If so, Have you been unconsciously tormenting yourself in some way?

ROOMS

Related themes:
Transition
Choices
Soul-searching

HALLWAYS & CORRIDORS

Perhaps you dreamed that you unlocked a front door, entered a house, and found yourself in a giant hallway. Like doors, hallways and corridors are places that we go through in order to arrive at other places; therefore, in the symbolism of dreams, they represent places of transition and choices to be made. And, as we mainly think of hallways as being at entry level, remember that the ground floor symbolically denotes the conscious mind. If you dreamed that you were walking down the hallway of your dream home, do you know where you were going or what you were looking for? And what was the mood of your dream?

NEW BEGINNINGS
Did you dream that you were walking through that hallway of a strange house and that you felt uneasy, lost, or upset? If so, have you been feeling "lost" in your life, so that you do not know where you want to go? It may be time for you to devote some serious time and energy into thinking about your life goals and how you might go about achieving them.

HOUSE & HOME

Related themes:
Spiritual life
Repressed memories
Heirlooms and keepsakes

STRUCTURAL FEATURES

ATTICS

Did you enter a dream attic? In actual life, this room is scarcely visited, but is nevertheless a repository for cherished items of sentimental value like journals, photograph albums, and clothes that we can't bring ourselves to throw away because they evoke such powerful memories. Despite the cobwebs that may festoon it because we pay it so little attention in our busy waking lives, the attic symbolizes rarefied consciousness and is a place of ideals and even spirituality. Did you grab a broom and start to brush away the cobwebs, thereby making sweeping changes? (Indeed, if you wielded any household implement in your dream, it's helpful to consider its function and relate it to something that's been troubling you.)

TREASURE

If you found yourself discovering a long-forgotten treasure in this room, does it remind you of an aspiration that you once cherished, but that has lain dormant because you've been too overwhelmed by the demands of working and family life to pursue it?

STRUCTURAL FEATURES

Related themes:
Instincts
True feelings
Fears

CELLARS & BASEMENTS

Did you decide to go down into your dream basement or cellar? If so, you probably descended the stairs with some trepidation, wondering uneasily what you would find there. In dreamland, these underground rooms symbolize the unconscious mind, where our "baser" instincts, energies, and urges are stored and where we conceal things that we would rather not put on display: possibly things about which we feel ashamed, yet cannot bring ourselves to let go of or throw away, but also items that we don't need right now, but may come in useful in the future.

INNER BEING
Wine is traditionally kept in cellars, and the contents of the unconscious can similarly harbor valuable treats that we bring out with a flourish for special occasions. Did you enter the cellar to seek out an issue that you either need to confront to find peace of mind, or else to bring to light, and make good use of, a bold quality that you've suppressed in waking life?

HOUSE
& HOME

Related themes:
Transition
Moving on
Social interaction

STRUCTURAL FEATURES

DOORS

Doors are transitional points that offer fresh opportunities. A front door usually admits unfamiliar influences, while a back door lets in people with whom we are more comfortable. Stepping through a dream door signals your willingness to embrace change, while letting someone in indicates that you are willing to interact with them. If you were faced with a bewildering array of doors, however, you could be feeling overwhelmed by a myriad of choices in life. And if you could not find any door through which to exit, this suggests a feeling of being trapped, but also, because a door can symbolize the mouth, you may feel unable to express yourself.

BEHIND CLOSED DOORS
Did a locked door make you furious or curious in your dream? If the former, your unconscious may have been signaling frustration that an opportunity seems to be closed to you. If the latter, is something being withheld from you in real life which you are longing to learn about? If it was a cupboard door, it may contain something that your conscious mind has suppressed: a "skeleton in the closet."

STRUCTURAL FEATURES

Related themes:
Vision
Vantage points
Voyeurism

WINDOWS

If the house is the "mansion of the soul," the windows are its eyes. If you dreamed that you were standing outside a window and observed a domestic scene with envy, it is likely that you are feeling in need of the comfort inherent in a close-knit family, a vital component of "home." If the window shed light on an aspect of the home of someone you know, it may alternatively be that you wish to understand them better. But if your dream home had no windows at all, or if drapes obscured the view, it is likely that you are taking a shuttered approach to life. Opening a dream window denotes a willingness to let some "fresh air" into a life that has, perhaps, become stale.

ENJOYING THE VIEW

Maybe you dreamed that you were inside a house looking out through a window. What did you see? Either a beautiful vista or a derelict landscape could denote how you regard life at present, but if this explanation seems unlikely, it may be that the former portrays the way you'd like life to be and the latter warns of a sharp downturn in your circumstances.

HOUSE
& HOME

Related themes:
Transition
Ascent or descent
Your outlook on the future

STRUCTURAL FEATURES

STAIRS

Like hallways and corridors, in the language of dreams, stairs represent movement, flux, or transition. Perhaps you climbed the stairs of your dream house to reach the next story. The second floor of the dream house represents a higher level of consciousness, beyond the day to day. Ascending a flight of stairs therefore denotes the following of your rising aspirations. If you found yourself descending a flight of dream stairs, this may indicate that you are at a point in your life where you need to explore the depths of your unconscious mind (perhaps by engaging in some creative or artistic activity). And, depending on the mood of your dream, it is also possible that your descent symbolized lowered aspirations, or intellectual or emotional decline.

UP OR DOWN?
If you found yourself coming to a complete halt on your dream staircase, and were unsure of whether to go up or down, are you pondering several options regarding your future, or do you simply have no idea where you are headed in life? Perhaps it's time for an adventure!

STRUCTURAL FEATURES

Related themes:
Protection
Stability
Imprisonment

WALLS & FOUNDATIONS

Did the walls of your dream house attract your attention? If so, how did they make you feel: were you securely enclosed or hemmed in and claustrophobic? Depending on the emotions that they aroused in you, your home's walls could signify either solid protection from the hostile forces without or unwelcome confinement. Whatever you decide that they represent, remember that they are walls that you yourself have constructed around you and that you have the power either to strengthen or demolish them. Take note of their color, too, because that may have an important bearing on the message of your dream.

SOLID GROUND

If your dream home represents yourself, what did your dream tell you about your foundations and walls? Were they sturdy and able to withstand all weather? If you dreamed that your house was built on subsiding land and your walls seemed in danger of collapsing, ask yourself if the values and relationships that underpin your life are in danger of giving way.

HOUSE
& HOME

Related themes:
Protection
Warmth
Security

STRUCTURAL FEATURES

ROOF & CHIMNEYS

Was the roof of your dream house intact, had it developed holes or, worse still, was it so rotten that it seemed on the verge of falling in? A sound roof suggests that you will be able to stand emotionally and spiritually firm when buffeted by the tempests that sometimes blow up in life; a leaky roof implies that you are increasingly being affected by the drip, drip, drip of some niggling emotional or aspirational irritation; and a dilapidated roof warns that the very structure of your life may be on the point of collapsing on top of you.

SMOKE & FIRE

Chimneys usually have one of two symbolic meanings in the dream world. The first relates to the hearth, the traditional heart of the home, around which family members gather at the end of the day. If your dream home had a smoking chimney, its smoke signal imparts a message that an atmosphere of emotional warmth prevails, but because a chimney's second symbolic significance lies in its phallic shape, it may also suggest sexual heat, or possibly an absence thereof.

OUTDOOR SPACES

Related themes:
Growth
Nurturing
Personal space

GARDENS & YARDS

Did your dream house have a garden? Considering its features will tell you whether you are successfully cultivating the seeds of your potential or are instead allowing them to become choked by weeds, as well as indicating how you perceive peripheral aspects of your life. If your dream garden was a floral paradise, it indicates that your endeavors have caused your personality to flourish. An overgrown, weed-choked yard, by contrast, warns that you have so neglected your personal growth that you have ceded control. Is it time to start nurturing your talents? Gardens are also very private places, so if there was a trespasser in your dream, does someone pose a threat to your emotional security in the real world?

PRUNED & PARED DOWN
Was your dream garden rather too tidy and somewhat sterile in appearance? If so, you may be taking an overly controlling, excessively organized approach to life, nipping something about your personality in the bud and thereby preventing it from flowering and achieving its full potential.

HOUSE & HOME

Related themes:
Rarely used skills
Peripheral matters
Concealed or stored items

OUTDOOR SPACES

OUTBUILDINGS

When we dream of houses, it's often an indication that we are thinking about ourselves, but dreaming about outbuildings suggests that we are preoccupied with matters that are on the periphery of our lives, such as the "tools" or transport that we use to maintain our appearance or lifestyles. A dream of going into a shed, for example, may be a sign that, in order to deal with a current life problem or situation, you will need to utilize some personal characteristic that you generally keep stored away. Depending on your actions, a dream garage can symbolize a period of stability, but could also signify idleness or staying home.

BARN DANCE

In the language of dreams, barns can symbolize those basic or "animal" instincts or urges that we may try to keep reigned in or shut away from the rest of our psyche, so if you dreamed of entering a barn, ask yourself whether you have a current need or curiosity to explore this side of your nature. Were there any creatures in your dream barn? If so, what were they?

STRUCTURES

Just as a house can represent you—your mind, body, and spirit, or your conscious and unconscious thoughts, your physical health and appearance, and your highest aspirations and potential—so other types of buildings can symbolize specific aspects of your personality (or else the personality of someone close to you) when they are the focus of your dreams. Remember, when interpreting your dream, that your sleeping reaction to the building contributes a vital clue to its meaning. That being said, the primary message that your unconscious mind was signaling probably lies in the purpose for which a particular structure is used in the waking world.

STRUCTURES

TRAVEL

AIRPORTS

If journeys in dreamland reflect how we are advancing in life, staging posts like airports often represent transitional points in the cycle of our personal existence. If you saw yourself in a dream airport, walking resolutely toward a departure gate, your unconscious may be hinting that it is time you waved farewell to this stage of your life and ventured off in a different direction. Any travel-related dream scenario may merely have reflected your conscious anticipation of taking a vacation, or your desire to do so. If this is so, but you dreamed that the check-in staff turned you away, are your ambitions being frustrated in the real world?

DEPARTURES

When decoding a dream that featured an airport, remember that, although they do represent potential new directions in the dream world, unless your dreaming self knew exactly where you were going, and thus which flight to catch, airports can also signify confusion and missed opportunities. In your dream, did you actually manage to board your flight?

TRAVEL

Related themes:
Transition
Safe haven
Self-discovery

DOCKS & HARBORS

If you dreamed of standing at a waterfront city's docks, and choosing which vessel to board, was your dream advising you to embark on a voyage of emotional self-discovery, or, alternatively, to actually book the cruise that you've long been meaning to take in the waking world? But if you dreamed of disembarking from a ship and stepping out onto the landing stage of a dream harbor, could the suggestion have been that you have actually embarked on a new phase in life, one in which your future will be markedly different? Consider that docks and harbors are places where the water (or, in symbolic terms, the unconscious) meets the earth (denoting the practical, conscious mind).

ALL ABOARD!
Did you dream that you were happy as you dropped anchor at a port or harbor? Might your unconscious have been highlighting your desire to "anchor yourself" in a loving relationship, or even in a particular location (particularly if you have been moving around from one place to another in the real world)?

TRAVEL

Related themes:
Change
Anonymity
Letting go

HOTELS

Did you dream of checking into a hotel? If so, were you charmed by its opulence and looking forward to enjoying its amenities, or did your heart sink at the prospect of staying there because it was dirty and shabbily furnished? If you are due to take a real-life vacation, your dream was probably reflecting either your excitement at the thought of temporarily exchanging your own home for a more luxurious one, or else your dark suspicion that you'll end up spending your nights in a dump. But if you are not consciously anticipating making a journey, could the implication of your dream have been that you have entered a transitional stage in life, and that the dream hotel (which is a home away from home and may, therefore, be a symbol of yourself) mirrored how you are currently feeling about your change of circumstances?

CLEAN SHEETS
Hotels are impersonal places run by others, so do you yearn for some welcome anonymity and lack of responsibility, or, alternatively, do you dread losing your identity and self-sufficiency?

TRAVEL

Related themes:
Change
Choices
Uncertainty

STATIONS

Maybe your dream portrayed you standing bemused and confused in a railroad station, unsure of where you should be going, but surrounded by people rushing off to catch their trains. Or perhaps your dreaming self was standing at a bus stop, letting bus after bus pull away rather than jumping onto any of them. Dreams like these may have mirrored your waking desire to move on in life, along with your sense of uncertainty regarding where to go next. Was your dream warning that your indecision is putting you in danger of "missing the bus," or letting a potentially life-changing opportunity, or connection, pass you by?

TICKET TO RIDE

In your dream, do you remember what platform or track number you were departing from? If so, does this number hold any significance for you (for instance, is it your age, or your lucky number)? Similarly, if you dreamed that you were purchasing a ticket for the next bus or train, your unconscious may have been reflecting your desire to "move on" in life.

STRUCTURES

TRAVEL

Related themes:
Direction
Your inner self
Sanctuary

TUNNELS

Was your dreaming self driving along a highway when you noticed a sign indicating a turn-off through a tunnel beneath a mountain? If so, did you decide to enter the dream tunnel, or to continue down the highway? If you chose the former option, your dream may have been highlighting your unconscious urge to depart from the route that you have been following in the waking world. And because mountains can denote towering challenges, and subterranean tunnels as passages through the earth symbolize the unconscious, could your dream have been indicating that you may be able to bypass the difficulties inherent in climbing to the peak of your ambitions by choosing to enter a transitional phase in your life?

DEEP DOWN
A dream of being in a tunnel may signify that, although being there may expose you to all that your unconscious mind contains (basic urges, uncontrolled emotions, but also innate wisdom), perhaps this will act as a catalyst, enabling you to emerge with a clearer conscious sense of your direction in life.

LEISURE

Related themes:
Fun
Chaos
Freedom

CIRCUSES & AMUSEMENT PARKS

Were you part of a circus act in your dream? Did you juggle, perform acrobatics, or walk the tightrope? Your unconscious may have been drawing a parallel with your reaction to your waking circumstances, and the reaction of the dream audience is also likely to have been significant. If you were a clown, do you feel that you are wearing a painted smile in real life? Or did a dream clown represent the archetypal trickster? Any chaotic circus or fairground scene may reflect that your waking world has become wildly disorganized. If you dreamed you were in a fairground, what ride were you on and how did you feel? Did a carousel mirror your sense of making no progress during your waking hours? Did a ferris wheel make you feel lofty and important? Was a puppet show playing-out a real-life scenario?

ROLLERCOASTER RIDE

If you dreamed of hurtling along a roller-coaster's tracks, are you feeling sickened by the dramatic emotional ups and downs to which you have been subjected in the real world lately, and are you longing to recover your equilibrium by grounding yourself in mundane reality?

LEISURE

Related themes:
Role-playing
Unreality
Confidence

THEATRES

Although a dream of watching a romantic movie or thought-provoking play may have been encouraging you to seek out love or intellectual stimulation in the real world, it may otherwise have been signaling that all is not what it seems in waking life. Did the cast of your dream play or movie consist of your friends and family? The business of stage and screen is illusion, so your unconscious may have been alerting you to a charade that those around you are performing in real life. We all tend to role-play during our waking hours, in order to make ourselves more appealing to others, so if you dreamed that you were acting on stage, how did the audience react?

IN THE SPOTLIGHT

If you dreamed that you were unwilling to take center stage, could your unconscious have been mirroring your reluctance to "put on an act," or to be the center of attention in waking life? Did you need prompting, and are you suffering from a crisis of confidence in the real world? Your dream may also have implied that life is not a dress rehearsal, and that it is important for you to "get your act together."

LEISURE

Related themes:
Chance
Risk
Destiny

CASINOS

The winning of certain games, notably those played with dice, depends entirely on chance, which is one of the reasons why dice have been associated with fate for millennia. So if your unconscious depicted you rolling a die and desperately willing it to show a six (a symbol of victory) in a tense dream scene, did it reflect your sense that your destiny is in the hands of fate, that the direction that your future is about to take is out of your conscious control, or that you are "dicing with death" in real life? Any dream in which you were gambling may have been warning that you are considering risking everything for which you have worked in the waking world on a chance and that the odds may be stacked against you.

JACKPOT!

If your bet on the roulette wheel won you a fortune in dreamland, could your unconscious have been encouraging you to set aside your natural caution and take a chance on someone or something because your stake (and the reference may have been to an emotional rather than a financial investment) has the potential to reap you rich rewards in the real world?

Related themes:
Knowledge
Retreat
New horizons

LIBRARIES & MUSEUMS

Did your dream place you in a library, where you scanned shelf after shelf of volumes looking for a specific book? Because libraries represent an accumulation of human knowledge and ideas, their inclusion in dreams suggests the pursuit of knowledge, be it to broaden intellectual horizons or to solve a waking problem. If you dreamed of pulling a philosophy book from the shelf, for instance, it may be that you unconsciously hunger for a deeper intellectual understanding of weighty existential issues. But if the book was a beginner's guide to plumbing, your unconscious may have been urging you to fix the dripping faucet in your real-life bathroom.

MUSEUM PIECE

Like libraries, museums foster knowledge by giving people the opportunity to study objects from the past that are of interest. When trying to decode the meaning of a dream that was set in a museum, any exhibit that caught your dreaming attention is of the utmost significance because it may have been pointing to something in your own past that has an important bearing on your present waking situation.

LEISURE

Related themes:
Choices
Empowerment
Wish fulfillment

STORES, MALLS & MARKETS

Stores are buildings of interaction, and as such, they point toward our basic requirements, the items that we consider objects of desire, and how well we go about obtaining these things. If you had a mundane dream of a supermarket, your unconscious may merely have been processing the memory of the shopping you did earlier that day, or else reminding you that this chore is on your "to do" list for tomorrow. Otherwise, could your dream have been indicating that you are successfully taking care of your fundamental need for emotional sustenance? Stores are buildings that offer a multitude of delightful opportunities, but also threaten potential exclusion and humiliation, and the dream theme should tell you whether you are feeling empowered or denied in the waking world.

SHOP 'TIL YOU DROP

If your idea of heaven is going on an extravagant shopping spree in real life, a dream of having a fantastic time doing just that is likely to have temporarily fulfilled your conscious desire to escape the tedium of your waking hours in the most satisfying of ways.

STRUCTURES

Related themes:
Nostalgia
Wisdom
Concentration

WORK & DUTY

EDUCATIONAL ESTABLISHMENTS

Was your dream of school or university simply reflecting your every-day life, or has it been several years since you set foot in a classroom? If the latter, it may be that your unconscious was pointing toward a past lesson that still has relevance today. Or are you feeling nostalgic about that period of your life when you were unburdened by the responsibilities of adulthood, or when numerous opportunities beckoned? If you had an unpleasant dream of school, it may be that you haven't yet resolved your feelings about a life experience you had there. Remember, too, that because these buildings are places of education, your dream may have been encouraging you to feed your intellect, learn a new skill, or express an innate talent.

QUICK STUDY
A dream school or university may have been reflecting your waking feelings of anxiety about how you are perceived or about how well you are performing in real life. It could also have been pointing toward your sense of restriction, and your consequent inability to spend your waking hours doing as you please.

WORK & DUTY

Related themes:
Routine
Pressure
Responsibilities

WORKPLACES

Did your dream faithfully re-create your actual workplace, thus mirroring your waking preoccupation with your job, or did you dream of laboring in circumstances that are completely alien to you in real life? If, in your dream, you were an assembly-line worker, do you feel that your sense of personal identity is being eroded by the people or tasks that control your waking hours? If you enjoyed a night shift in a factory, would you welcome surrendering your decision-making responsibilities in the real world? If you enthusiastically participated in some construction, could your unconscious have been encouraging you to give practical expression to your creative urges?

SORTED

Perhaps you dreamed that you were filing. Was this a comment on the mentally unstimulating nature of your waking days, or were you unconsciously stowing away memories that are no longer relevant to your daily life, but that you may wish to retrieve at some point in the future? Was your unconscious telling you to restore some order to your waking life?

STRUCTURES

INSTITUTIONS

Related themes:
Self-care
Fear
Being looked after

HOSPITALS & CLINICS

Unless you work in a hospital in waking life, you are probably grateful that you don't have to set foot in a healthcare center because to do so implies illness or injury, either because you yourself require medical treatment or because someone you care about is undergoing a health-related crisis. If you dreamed of being a patient in a hospital, was it a frightening experience? If so, are you actually worried about your health, and are you pushing your fears to the back of your waking mind? Perhaps your unconscious conjured up this dream scene to force you to face your fears, if only to set your mind at rest. Whatever the scenario, a dream that focused on a hospital and its staff suggests that you, or someone you know, is in need of some physical or emotional attention or tender loving care.

TAKING IT EASY

Did you thoroughly enjoy being fussed over by a team of kind nurses in your dream? Perhaps you long to be pampered, cherished, have your every need taken care of, to be made to feel important, and to be relieved of the burden of your responsibilities in the real world.

INSTITUTIONS

STRUCTURES

Related themes:
Judgment
Constraints
Guilt

COURTHOUSES & PRISONS

Unless you actually work in a courthouse, the appearance of a judicial building in dreamland often highlights either your feeling of being on trial during your waking hours or else a nagging sense of guilt about having broken a moral or social code. Were you filled with dread or stricken with remorse as you hurried past a forbidding courthouse in an anxiety-inducing dream scenario? If so, are you worried that your superiors at your new workplace will soon judge your waking efforts, find you lacking, and consequently let you go? Or have you consciously been suppressing a shameful memory?

BEHIND BARS

Any dream that confronted you with a place of imprisonment was probably drawing a parallel with your waking sense of confinement or anticipated loss of liberty. If you had a dream like this, ask yourself who, or what, is restricting your emotional, intellectual, or physical freedom in real life. Are you feeling trapped by the conventions of married life or by a dead-end job? Or has your own timidity locked you in a cell of your own making?

LANDMARKS

Related themes:
Aspirations
Aloofness
Loneliness

TOWERS

Because they are tall structures that soar upward, toward the sky, dream towers may denote "towering" spiritual or intellectual aspirations. Yet towers are also isolating structures, and your dream may have been commenting on your arrogance, intellectual aloofness, and unwillingness to abandon your "ivory tower" in order to descend to others' level. Or, was the reference pointing toward your loneliness and your sense of having become a prisoner of the unorthodox beliefs that prevent you from interacting normally with others? Freudian dream interpreters equate towering structures with phallic symbols, and thus also macho tendencies.

TOWER OF STRENGTH

Did you dream of being thrown about in stormy waters, in fear for your life, when you saw the steady flashing of an onshore beacon? A dream tower could represent a "tower of strength," or a person upon whom others rely for protection, support, and comfort, a symbolic association that may be especially pertinent if you dreamed that you saw a lighthouse.

LANDMARKS

Related themes:
Isolation
Protection
Boundaries

CASTLES

In your dream, did your unconscious show you barricading yourself into a dream fortress, desperate to hold the outside world at bay? Could it be that you have a real fear of being overwhelmed and defeated by a band of hostile aggressors in the real world? Or are you feeling so emotionally vulnerable that you are throwing up formidable emotional defenses to prevent anyone from breaching your façade (or persona), and thus getting close to the real you? Alternatively, did your dream highlight your self-imposed isolation from others, and the sense of security that you derive from being emotionally self-reliant?

HOLDING THE FORT

If your stronghold came under siege in your dream, could you identify the faces of the besiegers? If so, are these the people who have launched verbal attacks on you during your waking hours, or are they the friends and loved ones from whom you have deliberately withdrawn emotionally? Did your defenses hold firm in the dream scenario, or were they penetrated by the besiegers?

LANDMARKS

Related themes:
Decay
Desolation
Traditions and roots

RUINS

Though we tend to associate the idea of ruins with the remains of ancient civilizations, there are actually plenty of modern-day ruins to be seen in today's cities and towns. And if you dreamed of finding yourself walking the silent streets of a deserted or ruined city, did this abandoned cityscape mirror how you are feeling during your waking hours— namely desolate, lonely, and forsaken, with your family, social, and professional relationships in ruins? In interpreting your dream, you will want to consider what was ruined (i.e., the town that you grew up in, your first school, the city that you live in now, etc) and how it made you feel.

PAST TENSE
If you were calmly investigating the ruins of your grandparents' house in your dream, could this have represented the antiquated or obsolete ideals and traditions that your grandparents held dear and that they taught you as a child, but that are now of no value to you in your current life, except as subjects of historical or archeological interest?

LANDSCAPES

Dreams in which the landscape forms a significant backdrop to the action usually mirror your emotional reaction to your real-life circumstances, be they pleasant or trying. This chapter gives you pointers toward understanding dreams that feature landscapes prominently, but remember that it is also important to consider any personal associations that a dream landscape evokes. A sunny image of lazing on golden sands may have conjured up a vision of heaven for many people, for example, but if you consider a beach vacation mind-numbingly boring, this dream environment may have epitomized your idea of hell.

LANDSCAPES

Related themes:
Society
Community
Fitting in

URBAN SCENES

CITIES & TOWNS

Did you dream that you were wandering around a city or town, either one with which you are familiar in the waking world or one that exists only in dreamland? If so, did you enjoy strolling along its bustling streets, or did its atmosphere make you feel threatened or out of place? According to Jungian interpretation, population centers like cities and towns represent the community in which you live, how you perceive yourself as fitting into it, and how well you are getting along with others. So if your dreaming self relished the busy life and interacted easily with the people whom you encountered, it is likely that you feel secure in your place within your real-life community.

MEAN STREETS

In your dream, if the buildings that lined the sidewalks seemed to be closing in on you, or if you became hopelessly lost as you wandered the streets, the implication may have been that you are intimidated by others, trapped by your oppressive waking situation, and consequently fear that you are losing your sense of security, identity, and direction.

URBAN SCENES

Related themes:
Progress
Choices
Opportunities

ROADS & STREETS

A dream road or street can represent a way to get from one place to another—literally or symbolically—as well as indicating the stage you are at in your life journey. To dream of being stranded on a road without transport could imply a feeling of a lack of support in your waking life. A dream of driving off-road suggests a need to pay more attention to personal responsibility. If you are facing a difficult decision in real life, dream crossroads or junctions may be reflecting your anxiety about it. Similarly, a curve may refer to real-life changes, especially if you cannot see what lies ahead, but it can also refer to middle age and your feelings about "rounding the bend." Back streets may refer to an alternative way of life or a need to explore, and any road not taken may represent a missed opportunity.

LONELY STREET

If you dreamed of walking the silent streets of an empty town, are you treading a lonely path through the waking world, and would you welcome the companionship of a like-minded fellow traveler to lighten your journey and, if necessary, to hearten and encourage you?

LANDSCAPES

Related themes:
Fields
Sheep or cows
Nurturing or investments

RURAL SCENES

FARMS

In the language of dreams, a farm can represent a real-life activity where you invest time or resources for a long-term gain. So if, in your dream, you were growing crops or raising livestock, could this have been representing your waking pastime of managing your stock portfolio, for example? Did you dream of milking a cow, and of feeling enormous satisfaction as you collected bucketloads of warm milk? If so, are you currently making lots of money from a business venture during your waking hours? Remember that the individual animals which featured in your dream farm may well have had a significance of their own.

COLD COMFORT FARM

Consider the idea that the work of a real-life farm is entirely dependent on the change and cycle of the seasons. If the farm buildings of your dream were run down, out of condition, or generally left to decay, is your unconscious calling your attention to some area in the cycle of your own life? Do you need to take better care of yourself?

RURAL SCENES

Related themes:
Community
Nostalgia
Peace or traditions

VILLAGES

Like cities and towns, villages represent centers of community in dreams, but they differ in their size and setting. In interpreting your dream it is important to recognize what emotions you were experiencing. If, in your dream of a countryside outing, you came across a small, quiet community, consider whether it could represent a feeling of peace and serenity, away from the chaos of your urban life. Or, if your dream village was the setting for a market filled with the enticing scents of fresh produce and home baking, do you yearn for a return to a more traditional way of life in your waking world? If you were in a specific village in your dream, consider what comes to mind when you think of that place and its people.

VILLAGE PEOPLE
If, in your dream of a small community, you were dismayed to find an unfriendly atmosphere as people turned away from you, or a deserted village, are you feeling like an outsider in real life? Or are you perhaps feeling threatened by some looming issue which is affecting your closest circle of friends?

LANDSCAPES

Related themes:
Freedom
Sustenance
Reaping what you sow

RURAL SCENES

FIELDS

Cereal crops like maize, wheat, and rice — staple foods the world over — have a shared, and universal, significance when they appear in dreams, one that amplifies the message denoted by harvesting dream fruit. If you dreamed of wandering contentedly through an agricultural lansdscape and the gently undulating wheat fields of your dream appeared healthy and abundant, your dreaming mind was, no doubt, reflecting your optimism that you will reap a rich harvest, or rewards, for the emotional effort that you have invested in your waking ventures. Alternatively, a dream field with no distinct crop could simply represent freedom, remoteness, beauty, nature, or a feeling of being separate from society and its rules.

FIELD OF DREAMS
If the fields of your dream were blighted and sparse, you are probably unconsciously aware that there are hard, unproductive times to come. And if you were appalled to witness a crop devastated by a swarm of insects, your dream may have been alerting you the onslaught of problems you face in your waking life.

LANDSCAPE FEATURES

BEACHES

If you dreamed of emerging from the waves onto a beach, how did you feel after your swim? Were you refreshed and renewed, or exhausted and thankful to have found your footing? Beaches are places where the water (or, in symbolic terms, the unconscious) meets the earth (denoting the practical, conscious mind), so that leaving one for the other may have denoted your emergence from the changeable realm of the emotions and your return to the security of the rational world. Such a dream may, therefore, have signaled the end of a period of emotional introspection or turbulence in your waking life.

QUICKSAND

If you watched the water wash away your footprints in the sand, could this have reflected your desire to erase your past mistakes and problems? Or, if you dreamed of strolling along the dream beach and of being in danger as the sand started shifting alarmingly under your feet, could it have mirrored your worry that the solid foundations that underpin your waking life are starting to give way?

Related themes:
Emotions
Intuitions
Origins

LANDSCAPE FEATURES

SEAS & OCEANS

The largest, deepest, and most changeable of all bodies of water, seas and oceans harbor marine life and are believed to have been human beings' ultimate place of origin, too. As such, they can represent both life (and their saltwater, its essence) and the mother archetype. But when it comes to interpreting dreams focused on seas and oceans, perhaps their most pertinent symbolic association is with the unconscious mind, and with the ebb and flow of feelings that can sometimes build up into a tidal wave of emotional upheaval. If, for example, you had a nightmare involving a turbulent ocean, are your waking emotions equally tumultuous at the moment?

OCEAN WAVES

Did you dream of floating serenely in a sailboat? If so, it is probable that your life is untroubled by worries. Perhaps you dreamed that you then cast a line from the deck and waited for a fish to bite; if so, are you mulling over a dilemma during your waking hours? It may just be that your dream depicted you "fishing around" in your unconscious for a solution.

LANDSCAPE FEATURES

Related themes:
Drought
Isolation
Earth

DESERTS

Sand is often the only notable feature of deserts—arid, infertile, and desolate environments within which few creatures can flourish. So if you dreamed that you were crawling over the baking sands of an apparently endless desert, the fierce sun beating down relentlessly upon your dehydrated body, could your unconscious have been observing that your long-standing emotional isolation from others in the real world has left you feeling parched of love and affection? Could this dream also have been implying that you are longing to be revived by a long drink of refreshing water, a symbolic agent of emotional revitalization?

SCORCHED EARTH

If you dreamed of a desert scene, do you feel that your friends have "deserted" you in real life? In your dream, did someone give you the drink of water you'd been longing for? If so, your unconscious may have been holding out the hope that your period of emotional drought is drawing to a close, perhaps thanks to that person. Is he or she someone whom you are in contact with during your waking hours?

Related themes:
Abundance
Competition
Being trapped

LANDSCAPE FEATURES

JUNGLES

Perhaps you dreamed of trying to hack your way out of the dense, menacing foliage of a jungle or rainforest, dodging venomous snakes and insects as you became increasingly frustrated by your failure to clear a path to freedom. If you awoke sweating from a stifling dream like this, did you then have to prepare yourself to face yet another fraught day in the "concrete jungle," or your workplace in the city? Could your dream have mirrored your waking sense of being hopelessly trapped within an oppressive office environment, which you perceive as being a career hothouse filled with ruthless rivals, all doing their utmost to thwart your chances of success?

KING OF THE JUNGLE

In your dream, were you the "king" or "queen" of the jungle? Did you roar with delight as you swung by vine from tree to tree? And are you at the very top of the "food chain" in the jungle of your real-life corporate workplace? Perhaps you relish the ruthlessly competitive environment of your waking life, and this dream is simply reflecting your waking satisfaction and success.

LANDSCAPE FEATURES

Related themes:
Community
Being lost
Retreat or peace

FORESTS

Just as the unconscious sometimes uses the symbol of a single tree to represent you, so it may conjure up a group of trees in a dream scene to represent a communal environment of which you are a part in the real world. If you dreamed that you were lost in the heart of a dark, sinister forest, becoming increasingly panic-stricken as branches obstructed your way and thorns pierced your skin, are you feeling threatened or trapped at work, for example? Did you eventually emerge into the sunlight in your dream? Your unconscious might have been sending you a message of hope, if only you find the courage to take the steps needed to end your waking nightmare.

A WOODED RETREAT
Forests can be symbolically associated with the unconscious, so if you felt at peace in a dream forest, your dream could have been a reflection of your need to escape the demands of the outside world by retreating into your own inner environment for some much-needed self-contemplation and, perhaps, emotional recuperation.

Related themes:
Endurance
Ambition
Spirituality or intellect

LANDSCAPE FEATURES

HILLS & MOUNTAINS

Unless you consciously regard them as places of natural beauty or recreation, the appearance of hills or mountains in dreamland usually denotes either ambitious goals, whose achievement will prove difficult and daunting, or else the immovable problems that you will have to overcome in waking life. The unconscious also sometimes uses these land features to symbolize the course of your life, the first half of which you may spend striving to rise to prominence. Did you scale your dream peak effortlessly, or did you become exhausted, abandon the struggle, and turn for home? If the latter, are you seriously considering giving up on your aspirations in exchange for an easier life?

CRUISING DOWNHILL

Did you dream of descending a mountain with a sense of relief that the end was in sight? If so, your dream may have mirrored your conscious pleasure at returning to the undemanding reality of everyday life, now that you have proved your mettle by rising to meet the career challenges that confronted you.

LANDSCAPE FEATURES

Related themes:
Water
Floods
Feelings

RIVERS

In the language of dreams, rivers usually represent your feelings as you navigate your way through life, and specifically your current emotions. Was your dream river meandering or direct? The first scenario may have denoted the many emotional twists and turns to which you are being subjected in the real world, and the second, a straightforward emotional passage through waking life. If the water in the dream river seemed static, your unconscious may have been commenting on your lack of drive, while if it was flowing rapidly, dynamism may have been indicated. But if the waters were rising rapidly, are you feeling swamped by emotion during your waking hours, and unable to move decisively forward?

BRIDGE OVER THE WATER

Perhaps you dreamed of standing on a bridge spanning a river and observing the river rushing or flowing smoothly beneath you. The unconscious often uses bridges as symbols of transition, so could the meaning of your dream have been that you are at a turning point in waking life and that the events of the past are now "water under the bridge"?

LANDSCAPES

Related themes:
Floods
Water
Serenity

LANDSCAPE FEATURES

LAKES

Unlike those of seas, oceans, and rivers, the waters of lakes, lagoons, ponds, and pools are generally still, so if you dreamed of any of these tranquil bodies of water, could your unconscious have been reflecting your own calm emotional approach to waking life? If you were struck by the mysterious appearance of a dream lake, were you reminded of your own "hidden depths"? Alternatively, could your dream have been telling your conscious self that although you seem unruffled to others, deep down you are in emotional turmoil? Was anything moving around beneath the surface of your dream lake? If so, it may have symbolized the stirring of an unconscious instinct.

STILL WATERS

In your dream, did you dabble your toes in serene and inviting waters? Some dream analysts believe that lakes symbolize the womb. Could your dream have denoted your longing either to retreat to a safe haven, away from the difficulties of the waking world, or else your desire to be "reborn"? Or, if you are a woman, are you longing to conceive a baby?

LANDSCAPE FEATURES

Related themes:
Energy
Exuberance
Sources and origins

WATERFALLS & FOUNTAINS

Waterfalls, or rapids, and fountains are celebrated for the energy of their gushing, shooting, and tumbling waters, so if you had a dream of laughing with carefree exhilaration as you observed the awesome phenomenon that is Niagara Falls, for instance, your unconscious may have been mirroring your waking sense of euphoria. But why are you feeling so exuberant? Is it because your creative powers have suddenly burst into sparkling life in the waking world? Remember, too, that "fountain" is an alternative word for "font" and "fount" (see above), so that if you were captivated by a fountain's dancing waters in your dream, could it have been advising you to bring your unconscious knowledge or wisdom into play in a real-life situation?

RAW POWER
Some dream analysts believe that jets or torrents of water symbolize ejaculation, so if you are a man, and you dreamed of feeling exhilarated as you stood above a thundering waterfall, is your love life the source of your current ecstasy?

Related themes:
Safety
The mother archetype
Retreat

LANDSCAPE FEATURES

CAVES

Caves are the province of the archetypal mother, or Mother Earth, and may therefore represent the womb in the language of dreams. So if you dreamed that you were trudging through an inhospitable landscape, before creeping into the dark, welcoming warmth of a cave, are your waking circumstances so unremittingly miserable that you are longing to escape your problems and to beat an emotional retreat to the comfort, shelter, security, and oblivion of an all-embracing cocoon, a place where no one can get at you? If you are a heterosexual male dreamer, an alternative explanation is that your dream expressed your yearning for sexual fulfillment.

DEEP DOWN

Consider the symbolic association between the unconscious mind and the subterranean earth. When you stepped into your dream cave, or the realm of your unconscious, were you searching for an elusive insight, intuition, or memory that would help you to solve a conundrum that is currently flummoxing your rational, conscious mind?

LANDSCAPE FEATURES

Related themes:
Overview
Ambitions
Impasse

CLIFFS

Dream cliffs may represent many things, including ambitious goals or expectations that will be difficult to realize, hard-won achievements, or futility. Regardless of whether your dream depicted you making the ascent, did you find yourself standing on top of a cliff, basking in a euphoric sense of achievement? If so, have you conquered the obstacles that were standing in your way in the waking world, and do you now feel that you have reached a high point in your career? And as you looked down upon the dream scene, did you marvel at how small and insignificant the obstacles that you encountered on your route now seemed from your lofty vantage point

VERTIGO

In your dream, were you standing at a cliff edge when you suddenly became gripped by a fear of losing your balance and falling off? In this case, was your dreaming reaction reflecting your waking fear that, having attained your highest aspirations, you are in danger of losing the position, the kudos, or the financial rewards that you have worked so hard to win for yourself?

LANDSCAPE FEATURES

Related themes:
Protection
Separation
Being trapped

VALLEYS & CHASMS

Although they are all depressions in the earth, there is usually an immense physical difference between valleys, chasms, abysses, canyons, gorges, and ravines. Valleys are typically long, wide dips in the landmass that provide protection from the elements, so if your unconscious depicted your dreaming self walking in a valley, the implication may have been that you feel secure in waking life, albeit that your horizons may be somewhat limited. A sense of security is emphatically not offered by chasms and their ilk, however, whose deep, precipitous sides threaten to entrap and swallow up those unfortunate enough to fall into them.

ON THE EDGE
If your waking hours have been marred by conflict between you and your partner, and you dreamed that the ground opened beneath you, leaving you standing on opposite sides of an abyss, could this scenario have represented your dramatically divided viewpoints? Did you find a dream bridge, or did you remain apart?

NATURE: FLORA & FAUNA

If an animal featured in your dream, the crucial question to ask yourself is what you associate that animal with. Having identified the quality or, perhaps, "animal instinct," ask yourself how that may have relevance to your waking world. In the symbolic language of dreams, seeds and buds can signify potential; blossoms and flowers can denote an emotional, physical, or intellectual "blooming"; while a dream tree may represent the dreamer. Always bear any personal associations in mind when trying to work out what your dream may have meant.

NATURE:
FLORA & FAUNA

FLOWERS

Related themes:
Children
New ideas
Potential

BUDS

The unconscious sometimes uses buds to represent children, so a dream bud may represent the conception of a new life or idea, which, once made manifest, grows steadily larger until it reaches maturity, when it bursts into glorious bloom. If you dreamed of regarding a young, vigorous-looking bud with pleasure, could it have represented your daughter, who has just come of age? Alternatively, consider the possibility that the bud signified the early growth of your favorite project or brainchild. If you are actually childless, a dream like this may have been highlighting your yearning to become a parent in the real world.

DARLING BUDS

Did you dream of a cold spring morning during which you were enchanted to notice that a bush bore the first tiny bud of the new season? If the dream occurred during winter, your unconscious may simply have been mirroring your longing for the arrival of warmer days. Alternatively, was your attention being drawn to a budding relationship or your own latent potential, perhaps as an artist?

FLOWERS

Related themes:
Sun
Optimism
Innocence

DAISIES

Golden-eyed daisies (which also imply childhood innocence) and marguerites are both solar symbols that may signal sunny optimism and happiness when they feature in dreams. But if your dreaming eye was drawn to a daisy chain, this could refer to a series of connected events. For example, in the real world, have you recently met someone who is in a position to help you with a budding idea? Or, if, in your dream, you were sad to find a daisy that was rather withered, do you feel as if the "summer" of your life has passed? Perhaps your unconscious was encouraging you to face up to your own inevitable ageing.

SUMMERTIME

Did you enjoy a dream in which you were running joyfully through a field of daisies? Perhaps your unconscious mind was harking back to the carefree summer vacations of your childhood. Or maybe this is a signal for you to take more time to relax in your waking life, and to recapture some of your early, youthful enthusiasm and optimism.

NATURE:
FLORA & FAUNA

FLOWERS

Related themes:
Retirement
Sun
Autumn/fall

CHRYSANTHEMUMS

The late-flowering chrysanthemum symbolizes the fall season and harvest, as well as a happy, productive, or scholarly retirement. This is especially true in traditional Chinese belief. If you dreamed of a chrysanthemum, your unconscious may have been urging you to study harder for the exams that you may be facing in the real world. Japanese tradition associates chrysanthemums with the sun, and their unfolding petals are a symbol of perfection. In general, this flower signifies cheerfulness, and note should be taken of its color (i.e., red means love and white stands for truth). In Italy, chrysanthemums are associated exclusively with the dead, so for Italians, a dream featuring these flowers is likely to signify funerals.

MUM'S THE WORD

In your dream, were you carefully arranging a bunch of chrysanthemum stems in a vase with feelings of sadness or contentment? And do you consciously equate these flowers with anything in particular? Depending on your answers, your dream may have signified that you are anticipating a happy retirement or that you fear imminent death.

FLOWERS

Related themes:
Immortality
Aspirations
Spirituality

CLIMBING PLANTS

Ivy is an ancient symbol of immortality, because it is an evergreen that lives on in its full greenness throughout the seasons. Ivy and other climbing plants travel upward toward the sunlight, so a dream of one of these plants may also denote emotional or spiritual elevation, higher consciousness, or even someone who is a "social climber." Poison ivy, of course, may denote irritation or an annoyance. A dream of a house (a symbol of the self) covered in wild, thick climbers may indicate that you have been neglecting your personal care or emotional needs. But an ivy-covered church may represent your enduring spiritual attitudes.

CLIMBING HIGH

If you dreamed of a flowering climbing vine, such as a wisteria, sweet pea, clematis, or morning glory, consider the associations that you have with these plants. For example, was your unconscious mirroring your waking optimism, and the notion that life is sweet? Or is an idea that you have been nurturing now growing, bringing you close to its implementation?

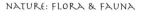

NATURE:
FLORA & FAUNA

Related themes:
Hope
Peace
Mourning

FLOWERS

LILIES

If you dreamed of a lily, but don't associate it with a funeral (when it may denote mourning and the afterlife) or a wedding (when innocence and hope are signified), are you a Christian? If so, the lily may have reminded you of the New Testament story of the Annunciation, when the Archangel Gabriel appeared to the Virgin Mary to inform her of her impending motherhood. If you are hoping to conceive, could this have been a wish-fulfillment dream, or was your unconscious advising you to follow Mary's example and be more compassionate to others during your waking hours? White lilies may also denote purity, truth, or compassion.

PEACE LILIES
If your dream lily did signify a funeral, it could have referred to a metaphorical death—perhaps the end of a particualr phase of your life. But if you are currently mourning a loved one, it is important to remember that lilies are symbols of eternity and the afterlife, as well as death, and your unconscious may have been reminding you to make room for peace and hope in your sorrow.

FLOWERS

Related themes:
Summer
Perfection
Miracles

LOTUSES

If the rose reigns supreme in the garden of Western symbolism, its counterpart in the East is the lotus, whose seemingly miraculous ability to flower within murky waters has caused it to be venerated as a cosmic symbol that unites the underworld, earthly world, and spiritual realm, furthermore representing death, rebirth, and enlightenment. In traditional Chinese belief, the lotus represents summer. It is sacred in ancient Egyptian belief, Taoism, and Hinduism, and is honored as a heavenly flower in Islam. Buddha is sometimes termed the "Jewel in the Lotus." This flower is also equated with the yogic chakras, or energy centers, within the human body.

MANDALA
If you consider yourself to be on a path toward enlightenment during your waking hours, then it is possible that your unconscious sent you an image of the lotus as a form of mandala to help you focus on your waking endeavors to transcend desire and suffering and to attain a state of nirvana.

NATURE:
FLORA & FAUNA

FLOWERS

Related themes:
Blood
Oblivion
Death and rebirth

POPPIES

The poppy is a narcotic-yielding flower whose symbolic association with oblivion, and hence death, dates back to ancient Greece, when it was dedicated to Hypnos (the god of sleep) and Morpheus (the deity of dreams). But the ancient Greeks also considered poppies to be symbols of fertility and love, and eating poppy seeds was thought to imbue one with health and strength. The poppy has become inextricably linked with death, but also with remembrance and rebirth, ever since blood-red poppies sprang up over World War I's fields of carnage, so if a poppy swayed gently in the breeze of your dream, could it have denoted your emotional numbness, or your poignant memories of a loved one who has departed this world?

TEARS OF LOVE
Greek mythology tells how poppies sprang from the tears of Aphrodite as she mourned for Adonis, and this made it a popular ingredient in medieval love potions. So did your dream poppy signify your waking desire to find a mate? Or did it point toward your feelings for someone in the real world?

FLOWERS

Related themes:
Love
Beauty
Romance

ROSES

Red roses are the classic Western floral symbol of love, romance, sexuality, and feminine beauty, and their symbolism has been elaborated on by countless poets and lyricists. White roses (which are often carried by brides) are a symbol of virginity, as are rosebuds, but because the red rose was sacred to Aphrodite and Venus, the Greek and Roman goddesses of love, a dream in which a red rose featured is more likely to point toward a man's sensual, red-blooded love for a woman. A yellow rose can be a sign of friendship and joy. But because this flower's stem is studded with sharp thorns, a dream rose may also be a warning from the unconscious of danger.

SMELL THE ROSES

Did you dream that you were wandering through a rose garden, feeling joyful and relaxed as you breathed in the sweet smell of the flowers? If so, your unconscious may have been advising you to slow down your fast-paced lifestyle and to take some time to appreciate the beauty of the world around you—in other words, to stop and "smell the roses."

FLOWERS

Related themes:
Neglect
Abandonment
Vigorous growth

WEEDS

As unwanted overgrowth in the garden of dreams, weeds may denote neglect of self or of one's personal growth, so that there is confusion or loss of control. Dream weeds may also symbolize an invasion of rogue ideas or foreign, unwanted influences, and a dream of being entangled in weeds may signify a waking feeling of being choked or suffocated, perhaps by the invasive influence of a dominant or charismatic person in your life. More positively, a fast-growing dream weed may represent a growing and developing child.

WILD LIFE

Dreaming of seeing a rampant, green weed growing incongruously among a well-regimented row of neat-looking bedding plants may have reflected how you are feeling during your waking hours. Are you feeling a little awkward and out of place, for example, perhaps because you have just left school, landed a job, and found yourself working in an office where everyone seems to behave in a neat and orderly fashion, except you?

TREES

Related themes:
Warmth
Family
Illumination

CHRISTMAS TREES

A dream featuring a Christmas tree festooned with glittering baubles and tinsel may have evoked comforting memories of heart-warming times spent with your family and friends, happy days that may seem far removed from your lonely life in the waking world. But if the dream tree reminded you of nothing in particular, it may be that you are unconsciously aware of its traditional, mythical, or religious symbolic significance, and that this may have pertinence to your situation in the real world. Some of these associations include eternal life (because it is an evergreen) and spiritual illumination and warmth (symbolized by the lights, which were traditionally candles).

FAMILY TIME

Christmas is such an important family holiday in the West that any yuletide dream may speak of your relationship with your nearest and dearest rather than of the birth of Jesus. So did the lights of your dream Christmas tree illuminate happy memories of Christmases past, or did they signal your dread of family fights and feuds?

TREES

EVERGREEN TREES

Because evergreen trees retain their leaves throughout the year, in dreamland they generally denote an "evergreen," or enduringly healthful and vigorous, approach to waking life. The laurel is an evergreen, and as the shedding of evergreen leaves is imperceptible to the human eye, early peoples deemed such trees symbols of immortality. So, if you dreamed of visiting a graveyard in which a loved one's grave was sheltered by a yew, your unconscious may have been highlighting its dual symbolism in both Celtic and Christian belief, namely of mourning, but also of eternal life.

ETERNAL LIFE

The cypress is a funereal tree, because it was once thought to prevent corpses from decaying, but, like many evergreens—or, indeed, any tall, thin tree—it may also be a phallic symbol, as may pinecones, which, being the fruits of evergreen trees, may denote feminine fertility, too. If you dreamed of a cypress tree, are any of these associations relevant to your waking world?

TREES

Related themes:
Seasons
Life stages
Strength

DECIDUOUS TREES

The ash, beech, birch, rowan, and hawthorn were all regarded as sacred by early European peoples, but it is the oak whose profound symbolism resonates the most strongly down the millennia. Dedicated to such gods of thunder and lightning as the ancient Greek Zeus, the Roman Jupiter, the Norse Thor, and the Teutonic Donar, the Druids designated the oak the embodiment of such masculine qualities as strength, solidity, and steadfastness, characteristics with which it continues to be linked to this day. So if your dreaming vision fell upon a venerable oak, was your unconscious advising you to stand firm in waking life?

LIFE CYCLE
If new leaves signify the development of fresh interests, whether personal or professional, withered foliage hints that these enthusiasms may be waning, and fallen leaves suggest that they are now things of the past. If your dream placed you in a wooded setting, and the leaves around you were yellowing, what might this mark the ending of in your waking life?

Related themes:
Creativity
Fertility
Sustenance

FRUIT TREES

Because fruits are the reproductive product of the trees that bear them, a dream fruit tree is likely to signify fertility, children, creativity, or new ideas or plans. Humans have long venerated fruit trees for the food that they provide, and likewise, a dream fruit tree may symbolize emotional sustenance, or else the harvest of a metaphorical "crop." And in Christianity and Judaism, the Tree of Life that grew in the Garden of Eden is said to have borne twelve types of fruit, which, if eaten, gave everlasting life.

FRUITS OF KNOWLEDGE

What fruit did your dream tree bear? As bananas may be phallic symbols, was a dream banana tree a reference to your sex life? If you are a Buddhist, did your unconscious conjur up a fig tree as a reference to the sacred bodhi tree, under whose shelter the Buddha gained enlightenment? Or, if you are Jewish or Christian, did your dream olive tree bring a sense of peace? Or did an apple tree refer to the Tree of Knowledge, and were you tempted to pluck a ripe and juicy fruit?

CREATURES OF THE WATER

Related themes:
Privacy
Defensiveness
The unconscious

CRABS

Because crabs and other crustaceans mainly inhabit the sea, they, like fish, can be associated with primal facets of the unconscious personality. Their armor-plated bodies also imply the wish, or need, to ward off outside influences, while their pincerlike claws can mount a painful counterattack if these creatures are menaced. So, if you found yourself confronting a crab on a dream shore, could it have embodied the "crabby," or bad-tempered, side of your nature that resists others' attempts to penetrate the tough outer shell that you've developed to protect your emotional core? And if its shell was broken, did this mirror your own sense of emotional vulnerability?

ARM'S LENGTH
Did the dream crab scuttle sideways as you approached and, if it did, did it mirror your own, or another's, tendency to take evasive action when anyone threatens to get too emotionally close to you in the waking world? Alternatively, can you equate the crab of your dream with someone who was born under the zodiacal sign of Cancer?

NATURE:
FLORA & FAUNA

Related themes:
Instincts
Emotions
Fertility

CREATURES OF THE WATER

FISH

In symbolic terms, large bodies of water are equated with the unconscious and fish are said to represent aspects of the instinctive mind, such as basic emotions or intuitions. The fish is also one of the oldest symbols of Christianity, so it may be that a dream of a fish was reflecting your unconscious craving for spiritual sustenance. Additionally, the elongated shape of many fish gives them phallic connotations, while, because the females spawn a multitude of eggs, fish are also symbols of boundless fertility. What was the dream fish? In Celtic lore the salmon symbolizes wisdom, and in Japan the carp is associated with endurance, courage, love, or good luck.

GONE FISHING

Did you dream of a goldfish bowl, or of visiting a dream aquarium? If so, your dream may have been hinting that different facets of your unconscious personality are being prevented from expressing themselves freely. Or, if you dreamed that you were fishing, this may have mirrored your unconscious efforts to extract a deeply submerged insight that would throw light on a waking problem.

CREATURES OF THE WATER

Related themes:
Instincts
Memories
Threats

JELLYFISH

If seas and oceans represent the unconscious, the creatures that navigate their depths can symbolize the nebulous thoughts and instincts that inhabit it. If a jellyfish drifted into your dream path as you were swimming, and administered a painful sting when you collided, could it have signified a memory that, although half-forgotten, still has the power to hurt you? Or did it gently drift past without harming you? Perhaps your unconscious mind was encouraging you to pay closer attention to your innermost voices and instincts in the waking world.

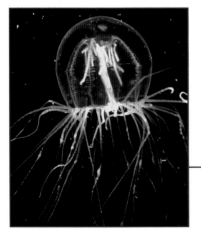

FROTHING SEAS

Many species of jellyfish are capable of congregating into large swarms or "blooms" consisting of hundreds or even thousands of individuals. If, in your dream, you were frantically flailing around, but found yourself trapped or held down by a mass of jellyfish tentacles, are you perhaps feeling confused by the turmoil of your emotions in the real world?

NATURE:
FLORA & FAUNA

Related themes:
Intelligence & friendship
The womb
Obesity

CREATURES OF THE WATER

WHALES & DOLPHINS

The whale symbolizes the womb, and thus also the mother archetype, so if one appeared in your dream, ask yourself why your unconscious could have conjured up its appearance. Are your adult circumstances so trying that you're longing to return to the warmth and protection of the womb, for instance? Or did the whale represent a terrible-mother figure who might be threatening metaphorically to devour you in the real world?

Dolphins have overpoweringly positive associations in both the real and dream worlds. Celebrated for their intelligence and friendliness, dolphins are reputed to steer to safety sailors whose ships are in trouble, and were once believed to guide the spirits of the dead to the afterlife, which is why the dolphin is a symbol of Christ.

DOLPHIN PLAY
If you dreamed of sailing through clear waters accompanied by an apparently laughing dolphin, you probably felt uplifted, but only you will be able to ascertain whether it held out the reassuring hope of spiritual salvation, or simply offered fun and friendship.

CREATURES OF THE WATER

Related themes:
Anxiety
Danger
Predators

SHARKS

The shark has the universal significance of the deadly predator, and when one surfaces on the waters of dreamland, its meaning is rarely positive. Sharks figure prominently in Hawaiian mythology. There are stories of figures that could change form between shark and human at any time they desired, and these creatures would warn beachgoers of dangerous waters. If a telltale fin loomed before you in your dream, was your unconscious alerting you to a dangerous or predatory presence in the waking world—perhaps even a "loan shark," someone who's recently offered to lend you money at an exorbitant rate of interest.

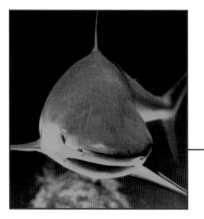

DANGER ZONE

A dream of an approaching shark is likely to have been an anxious experience at best, and a fully fledged nightmare at worst, for these marine creatures symbolize danger, destruction, and death when they glide into our sleep. So if you had such a dream, can you connect the shark with a vicious someone who is circling you hungrily in the real world?

Related themes:
Pearls and jewels
Defensiveness
Barriers and walls

CREATURES OF THE WATER

SHELLS & SHELLFISH

Did you dream that you were wandering along a beach when a shell caught your eye, and are you a man? Because shelled mollusks such as cowries and scallops can resemble female genitalia, it may be that your unconscious was commenting on the current state of your sex life. But if your dreaming self came across an oyster shell, was it closed or open? If it was clamped firmly shut, your unconscious may have been hinting that it contained a pearl, perhaps a "pearl" of wisdom, or else a female "pearl," maybe your ideal partner.

OYSTER FEAST

Oysters are traditionally believed to be aphrodisiacs, so could the message of your dream of a plate of fresh oysters have been that it's high time you pepped up your love life? Or was an oyster shell empty? If so, could your unconscious have been reflecting your sadness that life's opportunities seem to have passed you by, and your belief that the world is no longer your "oyster"?

CREATURES OF THE WATER

Related themes:
Wisdom and experience
Fertility
Foundations

TURTLES

The turtle's age-old symbolism relates to wisdom (due to its longevity and wizened face, a significance shared by the land-based tortoise), to fertility (it is a prolific egg-layer), and particularly to the cosmos (which many early cultures thought that it embodied, others believing that it supported the world on its shell). So, if you dreamed of watching a turtle lying helplessly on its back, frantically waving its legs in an attempt to right itself, could your dream have mirrored your waking sense that your real-life circumstances been turned upside down recently?

LONG LIFE

In Japan, the turtle is one of the four most prominent beasts, and represents the water element. It is known as *minogame* and is the most potent symbol of longevity and felicity. If in your dream, you were swimming happily alongside a friendly turtle, might this be an unconscious, happy indication that some recent decision of yours, perhaps with respect to your family life, has indeed been the correct one?

Related themes:
Mothers
Strength
Temper

ANIMALS OF THE LAND

BEARS

Because these animals hibernate during the barren winter months, could a dream of a bear have mirrored your desire to beat an emotional retreat from other people in order to catch up on some much-needed rest and recuperation? Or did it signal the need to batten down the economic hatches in order to survive the tough financial period that you are currently enduring? If your dream bear was bad-tempered, are you behaving the same way in real life, or is there someone, or something, that you cannot "bear" in the real world? If your waking hours are concerned with stocks and shares, could the appearance of the dream bear have denoted a falling bear market?

MOTHER BEAR

In times gone by, bears were imbued with powerful symbolism, their tendency to respond to any threat to their cubs with a fierce counterattack causing them to be especially equated with strength and the mother archetype. So if you dreamed of a bear and are actually a mother, could the creature have been referring to your powerful maternal instincts?

ANIMALS OF THE LAND

CAMELS

Because it is able to withstand long treks through the hot, dry desert without drinking any water, the camel is a symbol of stamina, patience, perseverance, temperance, and self-control. Could your unconscious have been using a dream camel in order to encourage you to trust in your stamina and to persevere in a difficult real-world endeavor? Or, as a camel stores fat, a source of sustenance, in its hump, if one swayed onto your dream stage, could its appearance have been a warning to start saving your resources in preparation for lean times that may lie ahead? In the ancient East, the camel was a symbol of royalty and dignity.

ENDURANCE TEST

Camels are best known for their ability to survive long periods without water in scorching environments, so it may be that your unconscious summoned a camel into your dream to reassure you that although you are experiencing an arid spell in your life—maybe your creativity has dried up—your inner resources will see you through it.

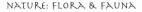

NATURE:
FLORA & FAUNA

Related themes:
Femininity
Independence
Superstition

ANIMALS OF THE LAND

CATS

Cats usually represent femininity in the language of symbolism. Also perceived as enigmatic, independent creatures, with astonishing survival skills (the proverbial "nine lives"), dream felines can denote feminine mystery, wisdom, and intuition. But when interpreting your dream, your real-life reaction to cats is crucial. If you dislike them, your dream feline may have represented a negative feminine archetype (the terrible mother, siren, huntress, or witch), an association that is underlined if you believe that cats are aloof, cruel, or evil creatures. Or is there a stealthy and deceitful woman in your life (maybe you yourself) who is behaving "cattily," or spitefully?

FELINE FRIENDS
If you like cats, and one appeared in your dream, it may have been a manifestation of one of the positive aspects of the female principle (the mother, princess, amazon, or high priestess), one that has pertinence to your life as a woman. But, if you are male, it may have been your anima, similarly guiding your unconscious attention toward a facet of your feminine side.

ANIMALS OF THE LAND

Related themes:
Camouflage
Fickleness
Change

CHAMELEON

If, in your dream, you observed a chameleon's skin slowly changing color until it blended in with the rock onto which it had crept, ask yourself if your unconscious may have been signaling the advisability of camouflaging your true feelings in waking life, or whether it was highlighting your fickleness. Or perhaps, instead, it was merely pointing toward someone you know who can change or alter their personality to suit any particular situation. In early Christianity, the chameleon was used to symbolize Satan who, like the chameleon, could change his appearance to deceive mankind. Is there someone in your waking life who you fear has fooled or cheated you?

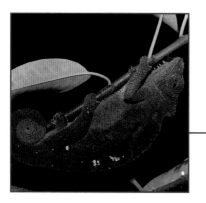

CHANGING COLORS

In Zulu mythology, Unwabu is a chameleon who was sent to humanity to grant immortality. He was too slow, and so we are mortal. It is said that the chameleon's color changes from green to brown because it is mourning Unwabu's sloth. Could your dream chameleon be a timely reminder of the inevitable?

Related themes:
Mothering
Cowardice
Pride

ANIMALS OF THE LAND

CHICKENS

The rooster, or cock, "rules the roost" and keeps his hens firmly in line, so if a cock strutted into your dream, it may have reflected either your domestic arrangements or else your "cockiness," or self-assurance. Cocks are also associated with lust, conceit, and boastfulness. Hens are said to embody the maternal instinct, so if you dreamed of a hen sitting drowsily on a clutch of eggs, could it have mirrored your own motherliness (or your yearning for children), or else your wish to be cosseted by a "mother-hen" figure in waking life? Alternatively, could your unconscious have been advising you against "counting your chickens before they are hatched?"

CHICKEN RUN

"Chicken" is a word that is used to denote cowardice, so if your dream concerned a chicken of indeterminate sex, your unconscious may have been highlighting someone's spinelessness in real life. But if your dream depicted a group of chickens, consider the implication that your "chickens have come home to roost," or that something you've done in the waking world is about to rebound on you.

ANIMALS OF THE LAND

NATURE: FLORA & FAUNA

Related themes:
Mother figures
Virility
Sluggishness

COWS & BULLS

Many ancient peoples venerated cows and bulls, and cows are still regarded as sacred creatures in Hindu India. In symbolic terms, milk-producing cows represent the nurturing mother archetype, so if you are a woman who is yearning to start a family and dreamed of a cow contentedly feeding her calf, your unconscious may have been reflecting your waking wishes. Bulls, however, are emphatically not placid creatures, and their fury is testosterone-fueled, which is why their symbolic associations center on masculine virility, might, and anger. If you dreamed of being charged by a snorting bull, might this represent a lusty figure in real life? Alternatively, if oxen featured in your dream, do you similarly feel that you are "under a yoke" when you're awake?

CHEWING THE CUD

If you dreamed of a herd of cows placidly chewing their cud in a field, could your dream have been mirroring the bovine, or sluggish and complacent, attitude that you've adopted when you're awake? Has your tendency been to go along with the views of the "herd"?

NATURE:
FLORA & FAUNA

Related themes:
Virility
Rivalry
Pride

ANIMALS OF THE LAND

DEER

Many analysts regard animals' horns and antlers as phallic symbols, and few creatures are more magnificently endowed in this respect than stags, whose association with virility is further compounded by their habit of locking horns with rival males and by their rampant sexual behavior during the rutting season, even though they are otherwise solitary creatures. But if you dreamed of a deer of nonspecific sex or age, could it have portrayed a gentle and timid "dear" in your waking life, perhaps even you?

STAGS

Pride, the masculine libido, and a tendency to confront competitors aggressively, but also to remain aloof from the herd, cause stags to be symbolically associated with young bachelors (also lending their name to prenuptial "stag nights," or bachelor parties). So if you are a man who dreamed of a stag, could it have symbolized your marital status, or your sexual behavior, or even your antagonistic relationship with male colleagues?

ANIMALS OF THE LAND

Related themes:
Loyalty
Companionship
Protection

DOGS

If a friendly dog romped through your dream, it may be that you are craving more fun and friendship in the waking world. Since dogs are traditionally regarded as faithful companions and protectors, it may be that your unconscious was either highlighting these qualities within yourself or else underlining your desire to have more support in the real world. But if your dream dog was intimidating, and if dogs make you apprehensive in real life, your unconscious may simply have been reflecting your waking fear. Or it may be that the dog represents a friend who is about to turn on you in the real world.

MAN'S BEST FRIEND

Dogs can represent friends in the language of dreams. So if your unconscious depicted you walking a pack of dogs, each straining so hard at the leash that you were having difficulty keeping them under control, could your dream have been referring to a waking struggle with your buddies? And if the pack did indeed break away, are you afraid of losing your friends' loyalty?

Related themes:
Foolishness
Burdens
Patience

ANIMALS OF THE LAND

DONKEYS

Although asses, or donkeys, and mules can also be ridden, humans mainly use them as pack animals, so if one of these beasts of burden plodded through your dream, have you been feeling weighed down by others' demands in real life? How did the dream donkey react to carrying its weighty load? If it trudged along uncomplainingly, the message may have been that you will, or should, exercise similar patience and stamina in dealing with your workload. But if the dream mule came to an abrupt halt and then flatly refused to budge, would you benefit from following its mutinous example in the waking world, or is some other person being as "stubborn as a mule"? Consider the puns: who is being "an ass," or foolish, in waking life?

BEAST OF BURDEN

Because they can be stronger and have greater endurance than horses, mules are desirable both as laborers and for riding. Therefore, if you dreamed of this animal, you may want to consider whether it represented strength, endurance, stamina, or a good work ethic; characteristics that your unconscious is perhaps encouraging you to adopt.

ANIMALS OF THE LAND

Related themes:
Memory
Large size
Stability

ELEPHANTS

Elephants are usually regarded as wise and friendly giants, who are also credited with the ability never to forget, so if this creature lumbered into your dream, could your unconscious have been drawing your conscious attention to any of these qualities within yourself? But if your dream elephant was an albino, could the reference have been to a "white elephant," that is, either a characteristic that you wish you didn't possess or an expensive venture on which you've embarked in the real world that you suspect may prove fruitless? Or, if a rogue elephant stampeded through your dream, could it have represented an antisocial quality within yourself?

KINDLY PROTECTORS

Among Hindus, elephants are considered to be the sacred incarnation of the god Ganesh. Buddhists consider light-colored or "white" elephants to carry special significance, and white elephants are revered as powerful spiritual icons across Asia. Therefore, if you are familiar with these traditions, could your dream elephant have held a spiritual meaning?

ANIMALS OF THE LAND

Related themes:
Cunning
Cleverness
The trickster

FOXES

Foxes have been associated with cunning for many centuries, and by numerous cultures. So if one slunk into your dream, could it have been alerting you to the need to outwit a real-life adversary? Or could your unconscious have detected some-one in your life being as "sly as a fox," a person who is "foxing" your waking mind with his wily tricks? Ask yourself who, or what, this devious trickster could represent (or was it the trick-ster archetype?), and then try to decipher the message from your unconscious. Alternatively, could the dream fox have rep-resented a "foxy" woman of your acquaintance, or, if you are a female dreamer, your own sexual magnetism?

UP TO THE OLD TRICKS

Did your dream fox appear as the shape-shifting trickster, the wild and rebellious maverick who acts on whim and impulse? If so, have you been tak-ing yourself too seriously during your waking hours? Was your unconscious encouraging you to be more like the trickster yourself—to let yourself be a little bit wild or silly, and to play more?

ANIMALS OF THE LAND

Related themes:
Fertility
Transformation
Unpleasant people

FROGS & TOADS

If a frog hopped into your dream, the message is likely to have been positive and concerned with a transformation. This association is derived from the frog's life cycle, in that it starts life as an egg, develops into a tadpole, and changes finally into a frog. This process of transformation is echoed by the fairy tale of the frog prince, whose human good looks were eventually restored by a princess's kiss.

Its hideous appearance, notably its warty skin and squat body, along with its habit of secreting poison to protect itself from predators, has caused the much-maligned toad to be characterized as a malevolent creature. So, if you dreamed of coming face to face with a toad, can you associate it with someone whom you believe to be a loathsome person in the real world?

FROG SPAWN
Frogs are symbols of fertility (due to the masses of eggs that they produce), so if you dreamed of gathering frog spawn, could your dream have been mirroring your desire to transform your waking life by having children, or else by adding to your family?

Related themes:
Power
Instincts
The unconscious

ANIMALS OF THE LAND

HORSES

Ever since humankind first tamed the horse for use as a means of transport, it has been credited with a number of symbolic attributes, including nobility. Its primary significance in dreams, however, is unconscious energy and drive, which, if the dream horse acquiesces, is controlled by the rider (the conscious mind), but which may buck against the rider's restraint if the steed is headstrong. So if you were riding a powerful horse in your dream, did you relish the feeling of being at one with your mount? If so, the implication was that your rational mind and your emotional needs are working in harmony. But if the horse tried its utmost to unseat you, this may have been warning that you are trying in vain to restrain an urge that will no longer be repressed.

HORSEPLAY

If you dreamed that you were on a horse that was running riot and refusing to be controlled by you, the rider, are your unconscious needs refusing to be bridled? Alternatively, you may simply have a conscious fear of horses and have been having a "nightmare."

ANIMALS OF THE LAND

Related themes:
Courage
Pride
Instincts

LIONS & TIGERS

Characterized as the "king of the beasts," the lion is said to be proud, noble, courageous, powerful, dangerous, and the embodiment of masculine strength. So if a lion suddenly turned tail and fled in your dream, could your unconscious have been signaling that your pride, courage, or strength is about to desert you? The tiger shares many of the lion's symbolic associations, but with the additional element of stealth. It also has a man-eating reputation, so if you are a woman who dreamed of witnessing a tigress prey on a helpless man, could your unconscious have been highlighting your own vampish tendencies as a sexually voracious huntress of men?

WILD BEASTS

When a wild creature enters a dream, it usually symbolizes a deep-rooted instinct, which is the "beast" within you. Further, the more dangerous the dream beast, the greater the danger that that suppressed aspect of yourself will break loose. A dream tiger attack could have indicated that you are in the grip of a ferocious rage that you fear unleashing in reality.

NATURE:
FLORA & FAUNA

ANIMALS OF THE LAND

Related themes:
Disease
Malice
Shyness

MICE & RATS

If you had a dream of a rat, it was probably an unpleasant one. Rats are associated with meanness and deception as well as dirt and disease. Could your dream have been about a human "rat" in your life — maybe a colleague who's been "ratting," or informing your boss about your minor transgressions at work? Or, could your unconscious have "smelled a rat," and was it trying to tell you that someone has been behaving suspiciously? If a mouse scurried into your dream, however, was the reference to your timid nature, or do you feel that someone in the real world is playing a game of "cat and mouse" with you, toying with your feelings?

POTIONS & POISONS

Rats earned their reputation for spreading disease during the Plague years. If you dreamed that you were confronted with hundreds of rats, are you afraid of contamination of some sort? Mice and rats both have associations with magic and witchcraft, and in particular, they are said to be witches' companions. Was someone in your dream keeping a mouse or rat, and are you threatened by her?

ANIMALS OF THE LAND

Related themes:
Mischief
Play
Obsessiveness

MONKEYS

If a chimpanzee was monkeying around in your dream, were you irritated or amused by its antics? Monkeys are renowned for their mischievousness. But mischief can be motivated by malice or playfulness, so depending on how the monkey behaved in your dream, your unconscious may have been alerting you to someone's tendency to revert to juvenile behavior in waking life, spreading chaos all around. Because monkeys arealso skilled mimics, could the implication of your dream have been that you are "aping," or emulating, another person in the real world? Or did you dream that a monkey had latched itself onto your back and that you could not shake it off? Could your unconscious have been referring to an unhealthy obsession of yours in the real world?

MONKEYING AROUND
If your dream focused on a colorful ape or an infuriating monkey that was playing tricks and causing mayhem, could it have been the trickster in disguise, an archetypal figure that your unconscious has summoned to tell you not to take yourself so seriously?

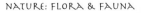

ANIMALS OF THE LAND

Related themes:
Greed
Laziness or selfishness
Contentment

PIGS

If you dreamed of a pig, hog, swine, or wild boar, what springs to mind when you first consciously focus on this creature? Greed and dirtiness? Or intelligence and friendliness? Pigs often provoke positive or negative reactions in people, but if you harbor no strong feelings about them and dreamed of a pig rolling uninhibitedly in the dirt, could your unconscious have been warning that you have been behaving like "a pig," that your behavior toward others has been uncaring? Have you been a "swine" to your wife? Or is your home a complete mess? Are you acting like a "male chauvinist pig," or are you being "pig-headed" in the real world? And if a boar blundered into your dream, are you being a "bore" and wearying people with the tedious details of your current obsession?

HOG HEAVEN

Pigs are not only negative in their symbolism. They may be seen as generous, unpretentious and friendly, characteristics of the Chinese zodiacal pig. The long-standing link between being well-fed ("porky") and being kindly and happy means that your dream of a piglet could have referred to a contented person.

ANIMALS OF THE LAND

Related themes:
Fertility
Shyness
Speed

RABBITS & HARES

In the symbolic lexicon of many cultures, the prodigiously fecund rabbit denotes fertility, this creature also being said to possess the characteristics of gentleness, sensitivity, and nervousness. So if a rabbit is featured in your dream, are you longing to be the parent of many children? Or should you perhaps be more kind and understanding in your dealings with others? Or have your waking circumstances caused you to feel transfixed with fear and indecision, like a shy rabbit caught in bright headlights? The hare is primarily associated with speed, so if one raced across the terrain of your dream, could its appearance have denoted your urge to streak ahead in life?

WHITE RABBITS

In the harsh real world, defenseless, herbivorous rabbits are the hunted rather than the hunters, and white rabbits are particularly vulnerable, as well as especially cute. So if a bunny hopped into your dream, could it have represented someone whom you feel is currently exposed to danger, and who needs your protection in the waking world? Or could your white rabbit have been magical?

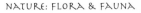

NATURE:
FLORA & FAUNA

ANIMALS OF THE LAND

Related themes:
Gentleness
Lack of initiative
Vulnerability

SHEEP

If you dreamed of being surrounded by a flock of sheep in a dream pasture, the message from your unconscious may be that you are not being assertive enough at work. If so, is it time to express your individuality, to break free of the flock mentality, and thus regain control of your life? The ram, or the male sheep, is wayward and self-confident, which is why its symbolic significance revolves around rampant masculine sexuality. Can you equate your dream ram with a a fear of men, or a particular man who is known to you in waking life, or, if you are male, with your own sexual needs? Otherwise, could this thrusting creature have represented someone born under the zodiacal sign of Aries?

LAMB TO THE SLAUGHTER

Lambs are traditionally associated with gentleness, innocence, and sacrifice. If you identified with a lamb in your dream, do you feel like "a lamb to the slaughter," that is, unable to resist the tendency of another person, or many people, to take advantage of your good nature, even though your acquiescence is now "killing" your emotional health?

ANIMALS OF THE LAND

Related themes:
Healing
Sins
Venom or malice

SNAKES

The snake is an ancient archetypal symbol that has both negative and positive connotations. If a snake or two appeared to your sleeping self, your unconscious may have been indicating that a process of physical or emotional healing has begun. But if you are a Christian, your attitude toward snakes may be colored by the serpent's tempting of Eve in the Garden of Eden, as well as its association with Satan. In this case, your dream snake may have represented someone who is trying to persuade you to deviate from the moral straight and narrow in the real world. Alternatively, as a phallic symbol, a dream snake could have denoted your repressed sexual urges (if you are male) or your sexual fears (if you are female).

SNAKE IN THE GRASS
Because it is a cold-blooded creature that either injects its prey with venom or crushes its victim to death, dreaming of facing a serpent that is poised to strike, or of becoming immobilized by its constricting coils, may have been warning of the silent danger posed by an emotionally ice-cold, venomous, or suffocating person in your waking life.

ANIMALS
OF THE LAND

Related themes:
Predators
Cunning
Isolation

WOLVES

The wolf shares some of the stag's symbolism in that it, too, can be a solitary figure, or "lone wolf" who lives apart from the pack, also being equated with masculine sexuality, albeit of a more predatory, deceptive, and stealthy nature. So if you are a woman who dreamed that you found yourself in Little Red Riding Hood's situation, could the dream wolf have denoted a male stalker in your waking life? But if you are a man who dreamed of a wolf, could it have been portraying your rather "wolfish" character? Whatever your gender, did you empathize with the dream wolf's solitary lifestyle? If so, do you wish that you could tread a similarly independent or self-sufficient path in waking life?

BIG, BAD WOLF

If you dreamed that you were pursued by a salivating wolf, but managed to rush home and set up a makeshift barricade, could your unconscious have been alerting you to the need to "keep the wolves from the door," or to take steps to protect yourself from the lean times that are looming in the real world?

CREATURES OF THE AIR

Related themes:
Peace
Hope
Togetherness

DOVES

Both the dove and the olive branch are worldwide symbols of hope and peace. The Old Testament records that, after the biblical floodwaters had subsided, Noah sent a dove from the Ark to search for dry land, which it found, subsequently returning to Noah bearing an olive branch in its beak. So, if a dove flew across your dream scene, could it have been urging you to make the peace, perhaps between feuding members of your family, or could it have been holding out the hope that the strife that characterizes your waking life will soon give way to harmony? If, however, a pair of turtledoves billed and cooed contentedly at each other in your dream, and you are single, it may be that you are longing to find a gentle, loving person with whom to settle down and enjoy a blissfully happy marriage.

DOVES ABOVE

The dove is a symbol of the Holy Spirit in Christian belief, so if this association resonates with you, could your unconscious have been pointing toward your desire for spiritual fulfillment?

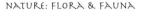

CREATURES OF THE AIR

Related themes:
Death
Greed
Threats

VULTURES

Vultures, ravens, and crows all feed on carrion, which is why their leading symbolic association is with death. So, if you were uncomfortably aware of being eyed greedily by a group of vultures in dreamland, do you feel that you have suffered a fatal blow in the real world (maybe because your business is on the verge of bankruptcy) and that the "vultures" are circling, waiting impatiently to feast on the remains? Alternatively, could your unconscious have chosen this bird to appear in your dream to draw your conscious attention to the need to "pick over the bones" of your failed relationship, or perhaps to "pick someone's brains," and thus gain valuable insight?

PICKING THE BONES CLEAN

If, in your dream, you watched hungry vultures tearing at the flesh of a dead animal and felt disgusted at the spectacle, did your dream self's reaction mirror the feeling of disgust that has recently beset you in real life, for whatever reason? It is important to recognize that the symbolism of such dreams may not have to do with death, but is more likely to represent the end of a period in your life.

CREATURES OF THE AIR

Related themes:
Wisdom
Witches
Nighttime and darkness

OWLS

Did an owl startle you by swooping noiselessly past your dreaming self? Or did you find yourself aware of a pair of "owlish," or solemn, eyes regarding you unblinkingly in your dream? The owl is usually regarded as a symbol of wisdom, probably on account of its large, piercing eyes and penetrating night vision. So could your unconscious have sent you a dream owl to mirror your wish to be guided through a murky real-life situation by a "wise old owl" or mentor? Or could the "wise old owl" have been a dream-world manifestation of the archetypal wise old man (high priest) or woman (priestess)? If so, did he or she direct you toward, and perhaps illuminate, a dark corner of your unconscious mind?

NIGHT OWLS

Because it is a nocturnal hunter that glides almost silently through the night sky, some early peoples branded the owl a bird of evil intent and associated it with death and witchcraft. And if you, too, consider the owl a "night hag," your dream might have reflected your waking fear of being the target of sinister forces.

NATURE: FLORA & FAUNA

Related themes:
Speed
Blindness
Intuition

CREATURES OF THE AIR

BATS

If you dreamed that a bat flitted noiselessly across a twilit dream sky, and you are afraid of these creatures, your dream may have expressed your intuitive feeling that you are actually about to be the victim of an attack from a sinister source. Otherwise, could your unconscious have been indicating that you are becoming "as blind as a bat," or else that your recent waking behavior has been "batty," that is, crazy? Alternatively, because bats are creatures that use sonar to detect their usual prey of flying insects, your unconscious may have been making a reference to your own heightened powers of intuition.

HIGHER POWERS

Bats are creatures of the air (which, in symbolic terms, is associated with aspirations and spirituality). And as mammals that have the rare power of flight, bats naturally have a certain amount of mystique about them. So if you had a positive reaction to a dream bat, it is possible that your unconscious was making a reference to spiritual elevation and enlightenment, or to the pursuit of goals and aspirations.

ANIMALS OF THE PAST

Related themes:
Primitiveness
Fear of monsters
The passing of time

DINOSAURS

Although they have been extinct for about 65 million years, dinosaurs do live on in our psyche—and when one of them (or any primitive animal) rears its head in a dream, the message from the unconscious may have to do with something that (or someone who) is outdated or out of style, with primal or "primitive" instincts or desires, or with a sense of pending doom (i.e., the threat of extinction). Or, if you had a scary dream about dinosaurs, do you feel as if some "monster" (maybe an internal one) is after you in the real world?

PAST TENSE

In recent years especially, dinosaurs have become a sort of cultural obsession in the Western world, due to the continuing discoveries of science, as well as to popular movies and computer games that simulate how these beasts may have looked, sounded, and behaved. If you dreamed of dinosaurs, was your unconscious simply reflecting a recently viewed documentary or movie? Or could it have been encouraging you to look into the past, for some reason?

Related themes:
Inefficiency
Age
Doomed projects

ANIMALS OF THE PAST

DODOS

The dodo bird is one of the best-known extinct animals and it is often mentioned in literature, popular culture, and everyday converstion in conjunction with a concept or object that has become out of date or defunct. Who has not used the expression "as dead as a dodo?" So, if one of these odd-looking birds made a surprise appearance in your dream, could it have represented the end of a relationship, or the "death" of a project? Alternatively, as it was a flightless bird, your dream dodo could have symbolized a person who is clumsy, ineffectual, or grossly unsuited to their purpose. Have your thoughts lately been dwelling on some such person in your waking life?

CONSIGNED TO HISTORY

As with many animals evolving in isolation from significant predators, the dodo was entirely fearless of people, and this, in combination with its flightlessness, made it easy prey. By the early nineteenth-century the dodo was believed by many to be a mere myth. If you dreamed that you encountered a dodo, have you been feeling insignificant, left behind, or at risk in your waking life?

BUGS & BEASTIES

NATURE: FLORA & FAUNA

Related themes:
The soul
Beauty
Flightiness

BUTTERFLIES

The butterfly represents potential made manifest. Did you dream of admiring a butterfly, and are you still (unhappily) at school? If so, your unconscious may have been indicating that you, too, will undergo a transformation once you have gained the freedom of adulthood. But if you are already grown up and you felt frustrated when a dream butterfly dodged your attempts to appreciate its markings, the reference may have been to your own restlessness. Remember, too, that a dream butterfly may represent your own soul or psyche. If one was flying free in your dream, and you are currently feeling overburdened during your waking hours, your unconscious mind may have sent you a dose of wish fulfillment.

FLYING FREE
If you have recently been bereaved, you may have felt comforted when a butterfly fluttered through your dream. Because the soul of someone who has died is traditionally said to take the form of a butterfly, your unconscious may have been signaling that your loved one's spirit has been liberated from the suffering of this world.

NATURE:
FLORA & FAUNA

**BUGS &
BEASTIES**

Related themes:
Predators
Traps or complex situations ("webs")
Abandonment

SPIDERS

Unless you are aware of the spider's ancient symbolic links with the cosmos and fate, a dream in which you were exposed to a spider is more likely to have been reflecting either your actual arachnophobia, or your waking helplessness when in the presence of a predatory, dominating person in your life (probably a woman, maybe a representative of the terrible-mother archetype). And if your dreaming self walked into a room that was obscured by webs, ask yourself how that particular room pertains to you. If it was a living room, for example, could your unconscious have been signaling that it's time to blow away the cobwebs and enjoy an active social life again?

CAUGHT IN THE COBWEBS

Because spiders weave sticky webs in which to entrap any hapless fly that alights upon them, if you saw a spider lurking in a dream web, it may be that your unconscious was alerting you to a trap that someone in your life has set for you (or maybe one into which you've already fallen). Alternatively, could a dream web have symbolized the complexities of your waking circumstances?

BUGS & BEASTIES

Related themes:
Plagues
Being outnumbered
Teamwork

SWARMS OF INSECTS

Honeybees live in colonies that we celebrate for their inhabitants' discipline when working for a common cause, so, if you dreamed of a "hive of activity," was your unconscious mind encouraging you to join in more at work? Or maybe you dreamed that you were forced to flee from a swarm of enraged hornets. If so, could the message have been for you to tread carefully, and not to "stir up a hornets' nest?" If you were stung in your dream, have you been emotionally hurt by someone's criticism in real life? And if you were appalled to witness a swarm of locusts, your dream may have been mirroring the horde of ugly problems with which you are being plagued during your waking hours.

REGIMENT OF ANTS

Ants are known for their industriousness and highly regimented teamwork. So, if your dreaming self observed a line of ants laboriously carrying a morsel of food toward their anthill, your unconscious may have been advising you to follow their example and to work in diligent and productive harmony with others.

NATURE:
FLORA & FAUNA

BUGS & BEASTIES

Related themes:
Pests
Ecological helpers (worms)
Self-sufficiency or slowness (snails)

WORMS, LEECHES, SNAILS & SLUGS

Although they are very different animals, worms, snails, slugs, and leeches share certain physical and behavioral characteristics and associations that render them somewhat close together in terms of dream symbolism. When they appear in dreams, they may denote slowness, lethargy, a person who is "slimy," or (with regard to leeches) a "bloodsucker." Snails will withdraw into their shells when menaced or sleeping, so if you saw this happening in a dream, do you wish that you could similarly retreat into your "shell" during your waking hours? If so, why? And if you are a horticulturalist who is currently waging a war of attrition on garden pests in real life, a dream that homed in on a voracious slug probably simply reflected your waking preoccupation with "the enemy."

SNAIL'S PACE
Snails are said to carry their homes on their backs, and they certainly move at a slow pace, so if you watched a snail inch its way across the dream stage, could your unconscious have been lamenting the length of time that it will take to repay your mortgage or renovate your run-down home?

WEATHER
PHENOMENA & DISASTERS
ELEMENTS
SEASONS

NATURE:
SEASONS & ELEMENTS

If the weather formed a significant backdrop to your dream, it is likely to have mirrored your current waking emotions; but remember, too, that your unconscious may have been forecasting an imminent change of mood. Did you feel unseasonably hot or cold while you were dreaming? And dreams of natural disasters can denote emotions that are so uncontrolled that they may have catastrophic consequences when unleashed in the waking world. Also, bear in mind that the cycle of seasons has its parallels with the stages of human existence.

NATURE:
SEASONS & ELEMENTS

WEATHER

Related themes:
Light
Heat
Power

SUNSHINE

The sun dominates the sky by day, bestowing brightness and heat upon the world, which is why it denotes intelligence and the illumination of the conscious mind, fiery, masculine energy, and, indeed, the life force. The daily (and annual) solar cycle is furthermore paralleled by the stages of human life, with dawn signifying rebirth (and enlightenment); the rising sun, increasing vitality; the midday sun, the height of physical and intellectual energy; the setting sun, the waning of these powers; and the disappearance of the sun from the sky, death. But if you were sunburned in your dream, it may be that you have exposed yourself to a dangerous situation in the real world.

SUNNY DAYS

Did your dream portray you lazing on a sun-drenched beach as you soaked up the solar rays? This may have reflected your radiant joy in life at present. If your waking circumstances are far from ideal, however, your unconscious may have sent you this dream to allow you to escape your conscious worries and to encourage you to keep your spirits up by implying that brighter times await you.

WEATHER

Related themes:
Happiness
Treasure
Transcendence

RAINBOWS

The magical-looking rainbow, with its beautiful palette of colors, carries the promise of happiness and treasure, or the pot of gold that is said to lie at its foot. It has also been regarded as a kind of bridge that links the earthly world with the divine otherworld. This association has prevailed in many cultures, including in ancient Greece, where it was said to represent Iris, the messenger of the gods. The Judeo–Christian Old Testament tells that God placed a rainbow in the sky following the flood as a symbol of deliverance and his covenant with humankind. So could your dream rainbow have promised riches, salvation, peace, or understanding?

DREAM COME TRUE

Once a dream storm had finally died down, and you had recovered your equilibrium, were you enchanted to see a rainbow arching delicately over the battered earth? If so, the message being transmitted by your unconscious was almost certainly one of hope for the future: that your dreams will come true "somewhere over the rainbow."

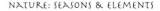

NATURE:
SEASONS & ELEMENTS

WEATHER

Related themes:
Gloom
Threats
Storms

CLOUDS

In the language of dreams, black, lowering clouds can signal the onset of a threatening episode or the dreamer's dark and pessimistic outlook—or both—while gray clouds usually denote despondence, and white clouds indicate contentment. Did some dark and heavy dream clouds shift slightly in your dream scene, allowing a shaft of sunlight to penetrate their dense cover? If so, and if you have been feeling sad or depressed during your waking hours, your unconscious may have been graphically depicting the ray of hope that may soon break through your gloom and lighten your waking hours.

DARK HORIZONS
Were you, in your dream, wandering merrily along on a bright day, singing joyfully at the top of your lungs, when a bank of black clouds rolled in and blocked out the sun? This scenario hints that perhaps you are unconsciously aware that your happiness and confidence in the future may soon be spoiled by a looming problem.

WEATHER

Related themes:
Tears
Cleansing
Relief

RAIN

If you were soaked by a downpour in your dream, how were you feeling? Were you miserable, or did you feel free and exhilarated? If the former, it is possible that an outpouring of emotions—your own or someone else's—is about to rain down on you, leaving you reeling from the onslaught. Alternatively, could the dream rain have symbolized the tears that you have shed, or wish that you could because they would provide some emotional release, during your waking hours? Or do you wish that your waking problems, or else the baggage of the past, could be washed away, leaving you feeling emotionally cleansed and looking forward to a sparkling new future?

SINGING IN THE RAIN
If you felt uplifted by a dream deluge, could it be that your waking life has become emotionally arid—perhaps because you are currently single and your work dominates your thoughts—and that you long for the moment when your ability to experience love and passion is refreshed and revived, so that you feel truly alive again?

NATURE:
SEASONS & ELEMENTS

WEATHER

Related themes:
Refreshment
Spirituality
Losing control

WIND

Because breezes arise from the gentle movement of the air, they share this element's symbolic associations with the life force, the spirit, the intellect, and well-being, and because messages are carried "on the wind," a dream breeze may have been signaling that breathing new life into your jaded mind would transform the quality of your waking hours. Perhaps the monotony of your working life has left you feeling mentally stale, in which case your unconscious may have been advising you to blow away the metaphorical cobwebs and become more free-spirited.

BLOWN AWAY

Any dream in which you were buffeted by very strong winds may have mirrored a feeling of lack of control through exposure to powerful external forces in the real world. Have you lately been forced to go along with other people's wishes? Or did you enjoy the sensation of being blown along? If so, do you long for an element of unpredictability in your waking world, or do you wish that you could relinquish your real-life responsibilities?

WEATHER

Related themes:
Attack
Threat
Exposure

HAIL

Hail forms when supercooled water freezes on contact with dust, insects, or ice crystals, and hailstones usually range from the size of a pea to that of a golf ball. Hailstorms can do serious damage, be it to automobiles, glass-roofed structures, or, most commonly, crops; and there have been occurrences of massive hailstones causing serious injury to exposed humans. It is no surprise, then, that dream hailstorms can be interpreted as being indicative of a real-life threat. Although rain can have positive connotations in dreams, hail usually sends a negative message, namely that you may be about to become the victim of a "hail" of bitter, stinging abuse.

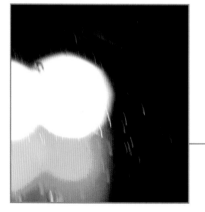

STINGING HAIL
Were you rushing along a dark lane in the freezing cold, in your dream, trying to get back to the warmth and security of your own home, when a storm of giant hailstones began to fall all around you? And did you raise your arms to protect yourself? Perhaps your unconscious is reminding you of a very real threat to your emotional security in waking life.

NATURE:
SEASONS & ELEMENTS

WEATHER

Related themes:
Coldness
Frozen emotions
Softness

SNOW

Because water is symbolically linked with the emotions, a dream that focuses on frozen water implies icy feelings. Can you draw a parallel with waking life? Are you emotionally frozen, or is someone in your life currently behaving "icily" toward you? A snow-blanketed dreamscape sends an extreme message. If you dreamed of being stranded all alone in a snowy setting, could your dream have been reflecting your own emotional coldness and isolation, or else the glacial atmosphere that pervades your interaction with others, or with a significant person, in your waking world? When pondering a dream like this, also consider whether the reference could have been to being "snowed under," or overwhelmed, by your work or studies.

SPRING THAW
If the snow was thawing in your dream, you may unconsciously have sensed that an icy mood that currently characterizes your waking hours is slowly warming and melting, and that your emotional life may consequently soon return to normal.

WEATHER

Related themes:
Confusion
Limited vision
Isolation

FOG & MIST

Dreams that are shrouded in mist or fog indicate that your conscious mind, or vision, is lacking in clarity, signaling in particular that you are unable to see an important situation, problem, or person, clearly, or for what it, he, or she really is. Both atmospheric conditions occur when water vapor condenses and is suspended in the air, and because water can symbolize the emotions, is it a myriad of feelings that is clouding your rational view, thereby making you feel uncertain about how best to proceed? But if the fog lifted in your dream, your unconscious may have been hinting that the confusion will similarly clear from your waking mind, revealing an obvious course of action.

GETTING LOST

Did you dream of groping your way blindly down your street, unable to discern any of its familiar landmarks or features because it was so heavily blanketed in fog? If so, your dream is likely to have mirrored your current sense of being confused, lost, and unable to make progress in waking life because your view of the path ahead is so hazy.

NATURE:
SEASONS & ELEMENTS

WEATHER

Related themes:
Release
Loss of control
Explosive emotions

STORMS

Whether they are depicted as taking place at sea or on land, dream storms usually symbolize overwhelmingly turbulent emotions. But consider the possibility that your dream storm represented a "brainstorm," or the unleashing of your unconscious powers of creativity, an interpretation that may be particularly apt if bolts of lightning sizzled through your dream. Could the flashes of lightning that illuminated the dark dream sky have represented flashes of insight or inspiration generated by your "brainstorm"? And did you awake from your dream feeling enlightened regarding a problem that has been baffling your waking mind, or else enthused by a new idea?

AFTER THE STORM
If you were fighting your way through a ferocious dream storm, you won't necessarily have woken up feeling exhausted, embattled and disheartened. Because all storms do, eventually, blow over, their appearance in dreamland could also imply that a threatening emotional crisis will at some point abate and that you can look forward to calm being restored. Was your dream storm over?

WEATHER

Related themes:
Chance
Destruction
Inspiration

THUNDER & LIGHTNING

Lightning can denote mental or spiritual illumination or revelation in the lexicon of dreams (as well as in Buddhist belief), but it is also a dangerous force of concentrated electrical energy that can destroy whatever it strikes, which is why ancient peoples regarded it as a manifestation of the awesome wrath of such sky gods as the Greco–Roman Zeus and Jupiter and the Norse–Germanic Thor and Donar. And if your dream scene was played out against a soundtrack of rumbling, cracking thunder, could these terror-inducing noises have represented the thunderous voice of an authority figure railing at your quaking self?

IT'S ELECTRIC!

If your dream portrayed you cowering on the ground as a firestorm of thunderbolts exploded above your defenseless head, could your unconscious have conjured up this image to underline your waking fear that, having angered an authority figure (perhaps your school principal or boss) in the real world, you are about to be punished for your transgression?

NATURE:
SEASONS & ELEMENTS

WEATHER

Related themes:
Destruction
Overwhelming force
Losing your bearings

AVALANCHES

Because avalanches dislodge masses of ice and snow, a dream in which one thundered its way down an icy mountaintop may have expressed a fear of bearing the brunt of someone's devastating emotional coldness (perhaps a spouse's) and the destruction of a close relationship in the real world. So, if you dreamed that you were engulfed in an avalanche, your unconscious may have been warning you that the foundations of your waking life are in danger of being swept away while you are powerless to stop them.

SNOWED UNDER

In your dream, did you glance up from your book and out of your window, and were you then struck dumb and completely incapable of fleeing as hundreds of thousands of tons of snow and rock came crashing down a mountain toward you? Consider the possibility that this dream avalanche may merely have mirrored your feeling of being overwhelmed by the "avalanche" of work that your boss has just dumped on you during office hours.

PHENOMENA & DISASTERS

NATURE: SEASONS & ELEMENTS

Related themes:
Upheaval
Destruction
Breakdown

EARTHQUAKES

Because the earth symbolically denotes the solidity and stability that underpins your personality, dream earthquakes signal that your emotional foundations are in danger of being shaken to the core, bringing the structure of your waking world tumbling around your ears and ultimately changing everything in your life. Can you make a link between your earthquake dream and an area of your life that may soon undergo an equally tumultuous upheaval? Have you (consciously or unconsciously) detected signs that you may lose your job, for instance, or perhaps even that a loved one is about to leave you?

AFTER THE QUAKE

If you were devastated by a dream in which you lost everything dear to you, remember that rubble is cleared away and buildings are reconstructed following an earthquake in the real world, so that if the worst happened and you found yourself jobless or spouseless, you, too, would rebuild your life, perhaps even emerging a stronger person as a result.

NATURE:
SEASONS & ELEMENTS

PHENOMENA & DISASTERS

Related themes:
Desert
Thirst
Water

DROUGHT

Since water is a symbol of the emotions, a dream where it is in scant supply takes on special significance. If your dream well dried up so that instead of yielding a bucket of cool, clear liquid, your winching actions were rewarded with dust, do you feel that your waking life is emotionally arid (perhaps because some emotional trauma has caused you to shut down)? And, since well-watered earth is essential for the growth of sustaining crops, if you dreamed of scratching around in a patch of parched, barren-looking earth, the implication may have been that you have become so drained by the demands of your waking life that your physical reserves have now become dangerously depleted.

EMPTY WELL

Water is collected and stored in reservoirs for communal use, so if a reservoir featured in your dream, could it have denoted your own emotional reserves? If you dreamed that the reservoir was in danger of drying up, are the incessant demands of others threatening to drain you emotionally dry in the waking world?

PHENOMENA & DISASTERS

NATURE: SEASONS & ELEMENTS

Related themes:
Chaos
Overwhelming emotions
The unconscious

FLOODS

Floods represent the destructive potential of surging, chaotic, and ultimately overwhelming urges and feelings. In the real world, dams can be constructed to restrict the flow of water, thereby preventing flooding. In dreams, dams generally signify the restrictive control of the conscious mind over unconscious instincts. If, in your dream, you saw a dam, was it structurally sound? Was your dream warning you that it may not be long before you "crack" under the pressure of your own rigorous self-control, and that once it has found an outlet, your unconscious will unleash the full force of its destructive power by overwhelming you with violent emotions?

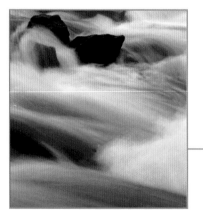

RUSHING RAPIDS

In your dream, was there a very fast-flowing river that rushed and rose before bursting its banks? Perhaps you have a real tendency to power and thrust your way through life, perhaps overwhelming, even damaging, those around you. Your unconscious may have been warning you to slow down and be more considerate to others.

NATURE:
SEASONS & ELEMENTS

PHENOMENA & DISASTERS

Related themes:
Anger
Devastation
Loss of security

HURRICANES & TORNADOS

Hurricanes spell danger in both the real and dream worlds, so if your dreaming self was assaulted by the full force of a howling storm wind, your unconscious may have been sending you an early-warning signal that it has detected a build-up of violent emotions, perhaps within your own mind, but more probably in someone else's. Are you about to become the target of another person's raging fury, did your dream mirror the powerful emotional conflict that you are yourself experiencing during your waking hours, or is a certain situation on the verge of blowing up into a crisis? A dream tornado may similarly have reflected your sense of being powerless to withstand a tempest of violent and chaotic emotions.

IN A WHIRLWIND

If you were caught up in a dream whirlwind, and were not afraid, but were instead dizzy or out of breath, are you spending your waking hours in such a "whirlwind" of activity that you're feeling confused and out of control, or was the reference to a "whirlwind romance" that may utterly change the course of your life?

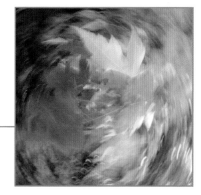

PHENOMENA & DISASTERS

Related themes:
Being swept away
Overwhelming emotions
Drowning

TSUNAMIS

The seas and oceans are the largest, deepest, and most changeable manifestations of water, which itself symbolizes the emotions, instincts, and urges of the unconscious mind. If you experienced a terrifying nightmare where you were deluged by a massive tidal wave or tsunami, it is likely that you feel as though you are drowning in a wave of emotions in the waking world. Have you recently received a piece of news about yourself that surprised, shocked, and panicked you? Or perhaps a close friend or family member has suddenly and unexpectedly opened up to you, revealing their woes, and sobbing uncontrollably on your shoulder.

DEVASTATION

If a tsunami completely wiped out the physical structures of your dream community, what happened afterwards? Did your people pull together to build new homes and hope for the future? Could your unconscious have been hinting at the need for a major change in your waking situation, in order for you to grow and move on?

NATURE:
SEASONS & ELEMENTS

PHENOMENA & DISASTERS

Related themes:
Release of pressure
Explosions of anger
Catharsis

VOLCANIC ERUPTIONS

Did you dream of visiting a famous volcano—perhaps Washington's Mount St. Helens, or Sicily's Mount Etna—and then having to turn and flee for your life as it suddenly erupted into fiery life, spewing molten lava in your path? If so, have you been struggling to suppress your mounting fury during your waking hours, and could your unconscious have conjured up this dramatic image to warn that you won't be able to contain your anger for much longer before similarly "blowing your lid"? Alternatively, maybe your dream highlighted your partner or parent's volatile temper, and your fear of being exposed to the full force of his or her rage when it explodes into your waking world.

LET IT RIP!
If you were bemused as the falling ash and lava of a dream volcanic eruption did not hurt you at all, and you perceive your dream to be referring to your own mounting emotions, remember that, although it is likely to be a difficult and painful experience, such a release of your pent-up feelings is likely to be cathartic.

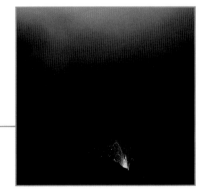

ELEMENTS

Related themes:
Flying
Ambition
Freedom

AIR

We may not be able to see it, but air is crucial to our survival, which is why it can be a symbol of life and well-being. A dream of choking may therefore have reflected the psychologically suffocating circumstances of your waking life. Because the sky is said to provide access to the heavenly realms, air represents spiritual aspirations, too, and through its association with "higher things," also intellectual aims and ambitions. If, during your dream, you were floating weightlessly, flying a kite, or letting a balloon drift upward, your unconscious may have been referring to your sense of liberation. But if you dreamed of a parachute jump, the implication was more likely to have been your need to escape a difficult situation in the waking world.

CLEAR BLUE SKIES
If you dreamed that you were floating in the gondola of a hot-air balloon and admired the view, your unconscious may have been advising you to look at the wider picture when trying to resolve a perplexing problem that is dogging your waking hours.

NATURE:
SEASONS & ELEMENTS

ELEMENTS

Related themes:
The unconscious
Emotions
Cleansing

WATER

In symbolic terms, water's primary association is with the unconscious mind, a significance that stems from our nine months before birth, when we were cushioned in warm fluid. This is also one of the reasons why we speak of the "waters of life," water being an element without which no creature can exist. In dreams and reality, water has the power to cleanse and purify (the spirit, as well as the body), as well as to relax and reinvigorate. A dream of water may therefore represent a desire to plumb the depths of your unconscious, a longing to wash away the "sins" of your past and be spiritually reborn, through a profound need to unwind, to a yearning for emotional or sexual stimulation.

WATERLOGGED
Not all water-related dreams have positive connotations, as you may have experienced if you dreamed of being deluged by water or in danger of drowning. You may have feared for your life, yet your dream was unlikely to have warned of physical danger, instead reflecting your sense of being emotionally overwhelmed during your waking hours.

ELEMENTS

Related themes:
Fertility
Sustenance
Stability

EARTH

If you are a gardener, you will know that cultivating the earth can reap astounding rewards, which is why the earth is associated with the bountiful fertility of "Mother Earth," also the giver of sustenance, stability, and security. But because the cycle of earthly life ends in death, when earth is featured in a dream, it may instead denote the culmination of a phase of your life. A dream of digging, feeding, or watering the earth may therefore have portrayed your wish to bring a new existence into being, while one of being underground may have implied a desire to undergo a profound transformation, the death of your old self enabling you to be reborn as a new individual.

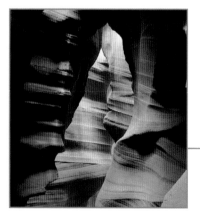

UNEARTHED

If, in your dream, you were lost in a maze of rocky arches and pillars or underground in caves, did you stumble across anything significant as you made your way out? If so, your dream may have provided you with the key to transforming your current circumstances, allowing you to live your waking life in the sunshine, not the darkness.

NATURE:
SEASONS & ELEMENTS

ELEMENTS

Related themes:
Destruction
Purification
Warmth or heat

FIRE

A potential significance of fire in dreams lies in its power to transform and purify everything that its all-consuming flames encounter. This interpretation may apply if your dreaming self felt strangely uplifted and relieved as you watched your possessions being destroyed in a raging inferno. A controlled fire, such as one that burns in the fireplace of a family home, creates a warm and cozy atmosphere, so that another possible interpretation of a fire dream points toward domestic contentment, or else the need for it. But fire dreams are perhaps most likely to be anxiety dreams. Your fears may stem from your own careless attitude to fire hazards or the presence in your waking life of an enemy whose anger has recently been inflamed.

A SINGLE FLAME

Did you dream that you were groping your way along a dark corridor when a figure approached, bearing a candlestick or lantern? Who was it? A dream like this may have signified intellectual or spiritual enlightenment, as a candle's flame illuminates its surroundings.

SEASONS

Related themes:
Birth
Childhood
Potential

SPRING

Just as the sequence of day and night is symbolically linked with the human lifespan, so the seasonal cycle can also parallel the course of human existence, so that each season represents a staging post along life's path. Spring is seen as a time of growth, renewal, of new life being born, and of the cycle of life once again starting. In dreams, spring may therefore imply birth and childhood. The seasons can alternatively signal your frame of mind when they form a backdrop to dreams, so that spring communicates a feeling of hopefulness and of beginning afresh. It can signal the start of better times.

SPRING IN THE AIR
If, as you dreamed, you gradually became aware of some tiny buds on the bushes, a hint of life in the trees, the faint sensation of warmth on your face, and perhaps a few early blooms at your feet, what was the context of your dream? Was there anyone with you? Perhaps you are developing new, "warm" feelings for someone in your waking life.

NATURE:
SEASONS & ELEMENTS

SEASONS

Related themes:
Maturity
Confidence
Well-being

SUMMER

While spring can imply new birth and beginnings in the dreamworld, summer can be seen to represent the prime of adulthood. This season signals a sense of confidence and of being at the height of your physical and creative powers—in your prime. Summer is also the time when schools, colleges, and universities break up at the end of the academic year, and is associated with vacations and outdoor activities. If, in the real world, you have been feeling "under the weather" at work or in your studies, might a dream in which you jumped on your bicycle and headed for the beach have been simple wish fulfillment?

SUMMER DAYS

In your dream, did you find yourself stripping off your outer clothes and leaping around the beach with a sense of total abandon? Did you feel enlivened as your body glowed in the heat of the summer sun? Could the sun of your dream have symbolized your desire for your waking life to be infused with a sense of contentment, freedom, or dynamic energy?

SEASONS

Related themes:
Midlife
Harvest
Empty nest

FALL

Fall signifies the maturity of middle age, fruition, and the reaping of rewards for past efforts. So if you dreamed of harvesting the last of your garden's crop of berries with a feeling of pleasure because you were looking forward to eating them, but also of melancholy because there would be no more that year, was your dream referring to a vision that you have worked hard to fulfill in the waking world (perhaps to bring up a brood of children), one that you are delighted to have achieved, although now that your work is done, you are feeling a bitter-sweet sense of loss (possibly because your children have left home).

FALLING LEAVES

Could your dream of sadness, as you wistfully watched the leaves falling from the trees outside, have been your unconscious reflecting your feelings about being in the "autumn" of your years? Or if you leapt about and kicked your way through a great pile of dead leaves in your dream, have you recently been satisfied with the fruits of your labor in real life?

NATURE:
SEASONS & ELEMENTS

SEASONS

Related themes:
Old age
Death
Hibernation or depression

WINTER

In the cycle of life, winter symbolizes physical degeneration and ultimately death. And the winter setting of your dream could signal your waking frame of mind if it communicates a feeling of retreat and decline. With its short days and long hours of darkness, winter for many people means a period of gloom. If you dream of being in a freezing and desolate landscape, have you recently experienced some sort if loss in your waking life, physically or emotionally? But dreams of this season need not always be negative, especially if you are an avid fan of winter sports. And dreams of a crisp, clear winter day could represent a much-needed break from a stifling atmosphere.

DEEP FREEZE

Winter is symbolic of, among many things, an absence of hope. Did you dream that you were alone in a winter landscape? Were you skating on a frozen river to which there was no end? Or were you snowed in, and feeling deperate in your abandonment and total isolation? Do you have a problem in your waking world which has increasingly been a source of frustration?

OBJECTS & ABSTRACTIONS

Our dreams may be filled with bright colors or obvious shapes, or they may resonate with piercing alarms or the sound of beautiful music, or else we may have been intently focused on a particular object or trying hard to solve an elusive riddle, so that we wake up with these on our mind, but are mystified as to their significance. In the language of dreams, colors, shapes and objects may have symbolic meanings, and dreams like these can be readily interpreted if we know where to look up the objects or abstract content to find out what they stand for, and thus to see the likely relevance to our waking world.

OBJECTS & ABSTRACTIONS

Related themes:
Depression
Spirituality
Intellectual clarity

COLORS

BLUE

If you awoke from a dream in which everything was suffused with blue, think back and try to identify whether this was a clear, soothing sky blue, a pale blue, or a deep hue. The connotations of each of these shades are quite different. If you dreamed of a sky-blue scene, you may have felt a sense of well-being, or else the color might indicate a connection with intellectual vision or a spiritual dimension. Pale blue may indicate the presence of a baby boy. Dark blue, meanwhile, is linked with the emotions, and in particular, though by no means always, with depression and "the blues." How did you feel in your "blue" dream?

BLUE MOODS

If your dream featured an abstract or swirling pattern of different blues, your unconscious was probably exploring your deep-seated emotions. This color may be equated with water, which is the element associated with emotions and inchoate feelings. Is there something troubling you that you have been suppressing—perhaps something you fear, yet should allow to surface in your mind?

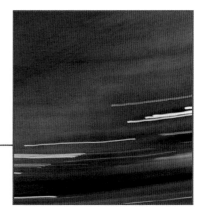

COLORS

Related themes:
Nature and environment
Jealousy
Immaturity

GREEN

A green landscape is one in which we can relax most read-ily and feel calm, because green is the color of nature, of vegetation and foliage. So if you live in a city apartment but dreamed of being surrounded by a lush tangle of green, or you were in an overgrown garden or forest, your dream may have been a reflection of your need to escape to a more natural environment, to refresh and recharge. On the other hand, green is also the color of immaturity and naivete, as well as of jealousy, so you should consider whether any of these associations may be relevant to your dream situation. Alternatively, was it a green light, or "go ahead," that fea-tured in your dream?

GREEN LIVING
The most important meaning of the color green is its natural association. If you were surrounded by green leaves in your dream, could you be feeling guilty about your lifestyle and your unnecessarily large carbon footprint? This dream may have been a reminder from your uncon-scious that it's time to look for ways to live more sustainably.

OBJECTS & ABSTRACTIONS

COLORS

Related themes:
Twilight (and "the twilight zone")
Spirituality and wisdom
Royalty and nobility

PURPLE

The color purple is seen at dusk, when the sky is neither light nor yet fully dark, and because of its link with this transitional time, purple has always been associated with mystery and spirituality. Long considered a royal, noble color, too, its association with royalty originated with the fact that priestly robes (and wizards' capes) were purple— and in earlier days, priests and wise men were the people who wielded power and were spokesmen for a higher authority. Was your purple-drenched dream concerned with spiritual or religious matters? Or perhaps with wisdom or compassion? Or, did you feel a sense of peace?

LAVENDER FIELDS

Dreaming of a sea of purple flowers may not have indicated a spiritual or regal association, but instead have been linked with something specific to the flowers themselves. If you dreamed of a field of fragrant lavendar, for instance, you may have been recalling a summer scene or yearning for the freedom of a summer vacation. Irises, on the other hand, symbolize hope, light, and communication.

COLORS

Related themes:
Earth
Practicality, common sense
Drabness or ageing

BROWN

The color brown is most strongly associated with the earth, so that a dream that was dominated by brown may have been a signal that you desire, ultimately, a more earthy lifestyle than you can find in your current urban, concrete-bound environment. Your dream could otherwise have referred to an earthy personality, or a sensible, practical approach to life. Have you been getting carried away with unrealistic daydreams lately, and do you need to come back down to earth? Or did you dream of someone you are close to being clothed in a brown cape or coat, and if so, is he or she trying to tell you that you need to be more grounded?

WOODWORK

Did your dream focus on a brown object, so that the object itself, as well as just its color, was significant? If you dreamed that you were contemplating a felled tree trunk, carefully counting its rings to assess its age, could this have been a warning from your unconscious that you are dwelling too much on the passing of time? Perhaps you need to "lighten up" a little and focus on life's colorful present.

COLORS

Related themes:
Passions
Romantic love
Blood and the life force

RED & PINK

Red is the color of blood, fire, and passions, and its prominent appearance in your dreams most likely signifies one of these meanings. Was someone in your dream bright red, or wearing red clothes, and could he or she be angry with you in the waking world? Have you done something to make him or her "see red"? Or, did you see in your dream that your spouse and your best friend were wearing red clothes or accessories, and if so, do you suspect that they may be having an affair in real life, or perhaps that they are contemplating one? Red is also a symbol of the life force, so that your red dream scene may have represented energy.

IN THE PINK

If your dream featured pink scenes, your unconscious was probably sending you a message that centered on well-being, and in particular, on romantic love. Have you recently met someone for whom you harbor strong feelings? Or has someone been hinting at romantic feelings for you? Alternatively, could you have been seeing the world through rose-tinted spectacles? Is it time to wake up?

COLORS

Related themes:
Sunshine
Warmth
Well-being

ORANGE & YELLOW

These are sunny, positive colors, because yellow, gold, and orange are all solar colors that bestow warmth, light, and contentment. Being in the sun makes us feel relaxed and suffused with well-being, so a dream that was drenched with a golden glow may have been concerned with vacations. Was your dream simply a wish fulfillment because you need to get away from your current situation and relax? If you dreamed of a yellow- or orange-clad person, the color may have symbolized their social skills. Someone with a sunny personality draws others to them effortlessly, and is often found at the center of a social circle.

BLAZING SUNSET

If you dreamed of a searing, hot sun in a parched landscape, was your dream mood cheerful or forbidding? A warm, relaxed mood in your dream indicates that your dream scene was related to your sense of well-being or linked in some way with feeling blessed, or "golden." If, however, the sun was oppressive, were you literally just thirsty?

OBJECTS & ABSTRACTIONS

COLORS

Related themes:
Depression
Dullness, lack of color
Elegance, sophistication

BLACK & GRAY

A dream that was filled with black is mostly likely to have been linked somehow with feelings of depression, death, negativity or hopelessness. If you have recently suffered the loss of someone close to you, your feelings of grief are likely to surface in your dreams for many months—perhaps years. If not, do you fear sinking into a negative state, and can you take steps to avert this in some way? On the other hand, black can also represent sophistication and elegance, so that if you were dressed in a "little black number" and holding court at a party, are you moving up in the world?

SHADES OF GRAY

The significance of gray can mirror that of black, so that it symbolizes depression and loss of hope, because something that is gray lacks brightness and color. If you dreamed of a dreary, cloudy sky, are you hemmed in by clouds on your emotional horizons? If so, can you find a way to bring some color into your daily life? Alternatively, shades of silvery gray can symbolize the moon, which stands for feminine intuition and creativity.

SHAPES

Related themes:
Life cycle
Climbing or striving
Love triangles

TRIANGLES & PYRAMIDS

Shapes are among the most powerful of archetypal symbols, but if you were dwelling on a particular shape in your dream, you probably woke up mystified as to its significance. Triangles have resonance as a divine or mystical grouping, for example, of the human mind, body, and spirit, or the cycle of birth, life, and death. If you were walking around the three sides of a triangle in your dream, could you have been contemplating this sort of triple grouping? Or, might your dream have concerned a "love triangle," or group of three people in an interrelated situation? Another example of this is a child with his or her parents.

PYRAMIDS

If your dream focused on a trip to the pyramids of Eygpt, or other, similar ancient structures, were you trying to climb up the sides? Are you striving to reach the peak of your potential? A pyramid can have cosmic significance, linking the earth with the heavenly realm. So, if you were looking up to its apex, could you have been contemplating something of spiritual significance?

OBJECTS &
ABSTRACTIONS

SHAPES

Related themes:
Stability
Foundations (physical or emotional)
Imprisonment

SQUARES, BOXES & CUBES

The square is a symbol of the earth, of solidity (as in "four-square"), and of balance and stability. If you dreamed of looking at something square-shaped, you may have been receiving a reassuring message from your unconscious that your emotional foundations are solid and reliable. Or, perhaps you dreamed that you were in a box, and you felt confined by it. If so, perhaps you are slipping into old-fashioned, "square" ways and becoming too rigid—or is someone else cramping your style and keeping you "boxed in"? Squares can also represent wholeness or completeness, because they symbolize the four cardinal directions.

SQUARE DANCE
Did you draw a square in the sand on your dream beach, and then did you stand back to contemplate it, and eventually wake up wondering what it might have meant? Because sand is shifting and impermanent, while squares represent safety and solidity, this dream was probably an exploration of your sense of emotional security. Does it feel like a struggle to maintain your grip?

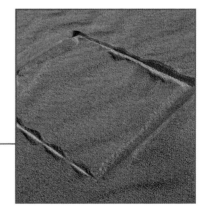

SHAPES

Related themes:
The self
The world
Harmony and balance

CIRCLES & SPHERES

A circle is a symbol of the whole self, in Jungian theory, synthesizing the parts of the psyche. This idea is also seen in the yin-yang, or tai-chi, symbol, which combines the positive and negative, the masculine and feminine, making a unified whole, in which each part also contains the seed of the other. So, if your dream was dominated by circles or spheres—perhaps if in the form of balloons or bubbles— could your unconscious have been telling you to work on integrating or harmonizing the conflicting feelings you have, so that you can achieve balance and calm? The same applies if you were meditating and contemplating a mandala.

GLOBAL WARNING

In your dream, were you holding and protecting a sphere or globe? If so, this could have represented your child or a project that is dear to you. Or perhaps your globe represented yourself, and you feel in need of some extra protection, possibly because something in your waking life is making you feel vulnerable at the moment. Listen to your inner voice!

OBJECTS & ABSTRACTIONS

SHAPES

Related themes:
Energy
Motion
Confinement

SPIRALS

Spirals may be seen as dynamic energy, such as is seen in the swirling water of whirlpools. If you dreamed of spiral shapes, could they have represented your whirling emotions, and perhaps a lack of control of your inner life? On the other hand, if you dreamed about a figure skater spinning rapidly and cutting a graceful spiral on the ice, the message may have concerned the skater's own positive energy and ability to maintain it with poise and balance. But if you dreamed of a downward spiral, your unconscious may have been sending you a message about the way you are heading in your waking life at the moment.

SPIRAL STAIRS

Did you dream that you were ascending a spiral staircase, and if so, how were you feeling as you climbed the stairs? If you were full of trepidation and felt enclosed by the walls, unable to move away at a tangent and set your own direction, can you relate this feeling to a parallel in your circumstances? On the other hand, if you felt comfortable, you may be set on a path to success.

PUZZLES & RIDDLES

OBJECTS & ABSTRACTIONS

Related themes:
Lost
Searching
Trapped

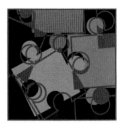

MAZES

If you found yourself wandering lost through a maze in dreamland, you may be feeling confused or "lost," without a sense of direction in life, during your waking hours. Did you fear that you might never find a way out, and could this fear mirror one that you've been suppressing in your conscious mind, about a situation you feel you can't escape? Alternatively, there may be something in particular that is eluding you and that you're trying to locate, perhaps via a tortuous route. Are you pursuing a goal—perhaps a new job or relationship? Another interpretation for this dream is that your dream labyrinth represented your unconscious mind, and your dream quest was a search for a buried memory or long-suppressed emotion.

TRAPPED!

In your dream, were you trapped in a maze with someone else, either a threatening stranger, or someone you know but wanted to avoid or escape? If so, the dream character may have represented someone whom you are trying to avoid, but may be better confronting to sort out whatever is troubling you.

PUZZLES & RIDDLES

Related themes:
Artifice, lack of spontaneity
Intellectual challenge and achievement
Mysteries and surprises

GAMES & RIDDLES

Dreaming of mysteries and riddles may be the result of your keeping a guilty secret in waking life. So if you were being given hints to a riddle by a loved one in your dream, is it possible that he or she has been withholding something important from you? If, in your dream, you were searching for the final letter in a crossword, or for the last piece of a jigsaw puzzle, could this symbolize your quest to find an elusive piece of information in waking life—perhaps a missing link in your family tree, or something at work that has been preying on your mind? Sometimes we dream literally of puzzles that are troubling us in our waking life, and on waking, may remember clues to the real-life solution.

PLAYING GAMES

In your dream, were you playing chess or backgammon with your partner or spouse? If so, the most likely interpretation is that you have been less than spontaneous with each other recently and your interaction has followed rules, as if you were playing a real-life game. Is it time to address whatever has made you behave in this artificial manner?

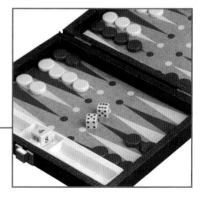

PUZZLES & RIDDLES

Related themes:
Problem-solving
Being lost or confused
Logical thinking

KNOTS

A dream knot may signify a number of different things, whether a "knotty" problem or something less obvious. Did you see a knot in a handkerchief or scarf, and might this have been a reminder of a task you need to do? Or could the reference have been to "tying the knot," or getting married, if this is something you have been thinking over. If you were trying to untangle a knotted mess of wires or ropes, or a mess of festive tree lights, could these have represented a convoluted situation in your waking circumstances? Perhaps you have been avoiding the obvious mess you've become embroiled in, and should sort things out.

STRINGING ALONG

Did you dream that someone you know was trying to untie a series of awkward knots on a rope or string? If so, was the person successful? This dream indicates that the person has some parallel issues to solve in real life. If the person was a stranger, could he or she have been your animus (if you are a woman) or anima (if you are a man), showing you one way you could try to solve a problem?

SOUNDS

Related themes:
Announcements
Seeking attention
Pestering or being pestered

KNOCKING & RINGING

In your dream, were you knocking on a friend's door? If so, was this your unconscious mind's way of reminding you to ask for something you want from him or her, but perhaps are reticent to bring up? Whatever you wanted in the dream, your knocking suggests that you were trying to get the attention of the person inside the house. Was it your spouse inside, and do you feel that you need to work harder these days to get his or her attention? Or, did the telephone ring in your dream, but when you answered, there was no one there? This dream could have been your unconscious "calling" to remind you of something you've put out of your mind.

RING MY BELL

If you dreamed that you heard a large church bell, gong, or similarly imposing sound, the ringing was probably to herald major news. Did you find out what the bell signified? If not, and you felt a sense of dread, is your guilty secret about to come out and be heard by everyone in town? Or, if the sound was welcome, are you ready to make a happy announcement, of a pregnancy or engagement, for example?

SOUNDS

OBJECTS & ABSTRACTIONS

Related themes:
Danger
Guilt
Denial

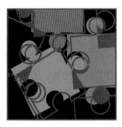

ALARMS & SIRENS

There is a literal interpretation if you hear an insistent alarm in your dream: is your smoke alarm ringing? If something as jarring as an alarm sounds in your dream, you are likely to wake up whether or not the sound is real. If the alarm was purely in your dream, was it a "wake-up call" from your unconscious, and do you need to come rapidly to your senses over something you've been foolishly ignoring or hiding from? Or, did you hear a siren and realise that the sound came from a dream ambulance rushing your son or daughter to the hospital? Dreams such as this may reflect guilty feelings of neglecting someone as a result of being caught up with other preoccupations.

INSTITUTIONALIZED?

Dreaming of a disembodied voice or alarm sound coming through an old-fashioned PA system may be connected with memories from school, or perhaps a workplace, where such a system was installed. In your dream, did the siren go off when you were trying to "escape" by sneaking out of school? If so, are you afraid of getting caught again now?

OBJECTS & ABSTRACTIONS

SOUNDS

Related themes:
Relaxation
Nostalgia
Expression

MUSIC

Music is a powerful means of expression, and if you heard music in your dream, the most important indicator of its significance is how the music made you feel. Was the sound romantic, joyful, triumphant, haunting, or funereal? Was it bassy dance music, and were you in a nightclub with someone you've been daydreaming of becoming romantically involved with? If it was a type of music you rarely, or never, listen to, perhaps the sound represented a point of view you wouldn't normally hear or pay attention to. Are you out of step with your teenage children, for example, and did the sound of their music seem more acceptable in your dream than it does in real life?

CLASSICAL SOUNDS

If your dream resonated with the sounds of a classical orchestra, and you don't normally listen to that sort of music, could the orchestra have represented someone with old-fashioned, traditional views? Has an older person, or one with more conventional views than yours, been trying to tell you something that you've dismissed, but should hear?

OBJECTS

Related themes:
Freedom
Independence
Finding a solution

KEYS

Keys are a symbol of freedom and independence and are often seen on greetings cards celebrating coming of age. Being given a set of keys to a vehicle or home implies that we are entrusted to use them responsibly. Did you dream that you were imprisoned, and you spent your incarcerated hours waiting for the jailer to walk by with the keys, hoping that you would soon be freed? If so, are you leaving the responsibility with others to show you the way out of your waking "cage," which may be an unsatisfactory job or a relationship with someone who is controlling you? If the latter applies, you would be wise to look for practical help.

KEY TO THE PUZZLE

A dream that focused on finding a key that you had been searching for may have had a parallel in your waking world. Are you looking for the answer to something, and could the dream have provided a clue as to where you might find the key to your mystery? Sometimes the conscious mind locks away a vital memory, but the unconscious mind releases it in a dream.

Related themes:
Anxiety
Pressure
Death

CLOCKS

Did you dream that you were packing for a business trip, preparing your files and samples, or else trying to cram your revision for an impending exam, watching the clock tick by and feeling pressurized, or even panicking? This is a classic anxiety dream, and frequently a recurrent one, which reflects some of the stresses of modern life. Clocks, too, are a symbol of our lifespan and the relentless way in which our time on earth ticks away. A watch or clock can thus be a symbol of death, just as a ticking sound can represent a steady heartbeat. So, did your dream timepiece highlight your feeling unfit or out of control?

CLOCKWATCHING
If the hands of your dream clock moved at an unnaturally slow rate, did you feel suffused with a sense of dread, or were you eagerly anticipating something that seemed as if it would never arrive? As ever, your feelings in the dream will provide the clues as to its interpretation. Watching a dream clock could represent the inevitable progress of your biological clock, too, if you are a woman.

OBJECTS

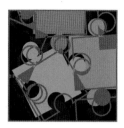

Related themes:
Alienation
Logic and consistency
Lack of emotion

COMPUTERS

In dreams, computers are sometimes a symbol of the mind or the brain, so that a faulty or slow dream computer may have represented something that is making you error-prone or tired and sluggish in your waking life. On the other hand, like robots, computers also symbolize an impersonal, unemotional way of doing or seeing things. Such faceless, repetitive, unimaginative approaches can be intimidating. Did you have a "conversation" with a computerized voice when you called your bank, in your dream, and did this leave you feeling alienated and frustrated? This could mean that you feel a lack of control of your circumstances.

BIG BROTHER

Did you dream that you were relaxing at home when you suddenly noticed that your laptop had sprung open and was performing calculations or recording messages by itself? If so, this may be a not-so-subtle sign from your unconscious mind that it's time to stop letting your work dominate your life so much. Or, is there some reason that you are feeling vulnerable about being spied upon?

OBJECTS & ABSTRACTIONS

Related themes:
News
Communication
Entertainment

OBJECTS

TELEVISIONS & RADIOS

Radios and televisions keep us informed about events in the world, as well as entertaining us. If you were focused on a radio or television broadcast in your dream, its meaning may be easier to determine if you consider your own listening and viewing habits. Do you use these media as a source of news, and did you see or hear disturbing news on your dream radio or television? In a dream, the broadcast may have been from your unconscious mind, and its news-flash may have been either direct (for example: telling you that you are overdoing things) or encoded. Do you remember its message, and can you relate it to your daily life?

NIGHT VISIONS

If you watched a horror movie before going to sleep, your nightmare of seeing scenes of bloodthirsty or suspenseful drama on your dream screen was simply your unconscious mind's way of processing scenes from the movie. But did you watch a soap opera in your dream? If so, can you relate its characters or the scenarios to your life? Or were you watching a blank screen, and if so, do you need to develop new interests?

OBJECTS

Related themes:
Aimlessness
Getting lost
Changing direction

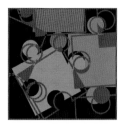

MAPS

Dreams that involve poring over maps often indicate that we are looking for directions in the journey of life. If you dreamed that you were walking or driving somewhere in a familiar place, yet you were becoming increasingly anxious that you had lost your way, did you consult a map? If so, there may be a parallel in your waking circumstances. You may be "going around in circles" or "losing your way" and need to think through where you are heading. Your dream map may have been your unconscious mind's way of telling you to step back and try to work out a constructive plan instead of continuing aimlessly as you have been.

NEW TERRITORY

Did you dream that you were on an adventure vacation, with no particular plan or deadline, simply traveling from one place to another, with an open mind as to where on the map you should explore next? This may have been a wish-fulfillment dream if you have been feeling limited and tied down in your waking world. Or it could have been the encouragement you need to "branch out."

OBJECTS &
ABSTRACTIONS

Related themes:
Identity
Independence
Freedom

PASSPORTS & TICKETS

In your dream, did you present your passport to an official, who promptly took it away and left you nervous that you wouldn't be able to get it back? In the language of dreams, travel documents can have a similar significance to that of keys—independence and freedom of movement. Without your passport, you can be held hostage. Or could someone have been trying to steal your identity, and may that person have represented someone in your office who has tried to take credit for your work or your ideas? On the other hand, if your dream depicted you gathering your passport and tickets to set off on vacation, is it time you took one?

MISTAKEN IDENTITY

If you dreamed that you were ready to present your passport when you realised that it was not yours, how did it make you feel? Were you excited, and are you subconsciously yearning for someone else's life because your own has become intolerable, or maybe just too boring? If you were frightened, however, there may be a lurking threat in your waking life that is manifesting itself in your dream.

CREATURES & BEINGS
RELIGION & REALMS
FESTIVALS & RITES
SPECIAL POWERS

SPIRITUALITY, MAGIC & MYTH

When interpreting any dream of a religious or spiritual nature, it is crucial to take your own beliefs (or lack of them) into consideration. The key to its meaning lies in what the figure, ritual, or object that you dreamed of represents to you. Similarly, if your dream was of magical happenings and creatures, what is your attitude to them in waking life? Do you believe in magic and the supernatural, and if so, do you consider these as dark and evil or benevolent? If you dreamed of monsters and mythical creatures, these may have represented your own phobias and desires.

CREATURES & BEINGS

Related themes:
Intermediary or messenger
Protection
Spiritual presence

ANGELS

Angels are among the perfect beings of spiritual and religious belief systems that possess a level of purity that lifts them far above the flawed world of humanity. These beings embody positive qualities to which we can try to aspire, even though we will inevitably fall short. Because angels and similar immortals are traditionally considered to be messengers between the world above and our own, your dream angel may have appeared to remind you that your behavior toward someone falls short of your usual moral standards. Or, your guardian angel may have been trying to deliver an important message concerning a threat you face in life.

WATCHING OVER YOU

If you dreamed of an angel on a headstone or memorial to someone close whom you have lost, could the message from your unconscious mind have been to point out to you how your lost spouse, friend, or sibling would have coped with a difficult situation you find yourself in? Dreams like this can leave us with a comforting sense of being watched over with kindnesss by the departed.

CREATURES & BEINGS

SPIRITUALITY, MAGIC & MYTH

Related themes:
Departed loved ones
Repressed memories
Fears and guilty secrets

GHOSTS

If you dreamed of a ghostly presence that made you feel afraid or uncomfortable, it could have been a reminder from your unconscious of something that has plagued you in the past, or else given you a guilty conscience. On the other hand, a dream of a ghostly figure whom you identified as a family member or friend who has long since died may have been a comforting experience, giving you the feeling that the person is still, on some level, "with you." Did the apparition have a message for you, or was it just a passive presence? These dreams occur quite frequently, whether or not the dreamer believes in the existence of ghosts.

SHADOW FIGURES
If your dream featured a shadowy scene that you could later identify as a place you are familiar with, how did you feel in the dream? On waking, ask yourself if the location means something to you. Have you been there before, and has something happened recently that could have triggered a repressed memory? Or was it a scene resembling a classic night-mare, such as a deserted cemetery?

SPIRITUAL & MYTHICAL

CREATURES & BEINGS

MONSTERS

Monsters populate our nightmares from a young age and plague us more during childhood than as adults. Fairy tales, children's stories and horror films often tell of monsters, archetypal terrifying creatures that must be slain (usually by the young hero who must earn his status as an adult) before they can prey on vulnerable humans. If we have dreams of monsters in adulthood, the monsters are likely to represent our own fears, whether conscious or not. If you dream of the same monster repeatedly, it may be worth searching your memory for clues as to how to "slay" it, or address the deep-seated fear at the root of your nightmares.

DRAGONS

The mythical dragon, a winged serpent, has symbolism that you must interpret according to your cultural heritage. It is revered as a bringer of good fortune and a protector in some cultures, but as the embodiment of Satan by Christians, while some psychologists say that it is an embodiment of the terrible mother, the human "dragon." Did one of these dragons feature in your dream?

CREATURES & BEINGS

SPIRITUALITY, MAGIC & MYTH

Related themes:
Seduction
Independence
Annihilation

MERMAIDS

As beautiful as mermaids usually are in fairy tales and legends, these mythological creatures bring heartbreak or total ruin to the men they entrance. If you are a man who dreamed of a seductive mermaid, did you swim after her, but fail to catch up with her? If so, did she have the face of a woman to whom you are irresistibly attracted in real life? Your unconscious may be alerting you that, deep down, you recognize that she may hurt you profoundly if you mistake her attentions for genuine feelings. Or, have you been hurt too often, and do you view all women as treacherous?

FREE SPIRIT

If you are a woman who dreamed that you were a mermaid, could this have related to your unwillingness to commit yourself to someone in a relationship? In our society, this is more often seen as a male characteristic, but many women feel reluctant to let go of the freedom and independence of single life. Or, if you were swimming through the deep sea, you may have been exploring the waters of your deepest emotions.

CREATURES & BEINGS

Related themes:
Fate
Fantasy
Magic

FAIRIES & ELVES

Elves, fairies, and imps are fantastical creatures who possess magical powers, though they tend to be small, and their powers are similarly limited. Fairies are popularly believed to help us, sometimes in the form of our own, personal "fairy godmother." If your guardian fairy came to your aid to solve a problem that is plaguing you, you had a wish-fulfillment dream—possibly in the graphic form of granting you a specific dream wish. But if imps or elves were causing mischief and disrupting you, do you feel as though things are slipping beyond your control in your waking life, and do you feel as though you are being targeted for bad luck?

FAIRY GODMOTHER

Did your fairy godmother appear in your dream and promise to grant your wishes with a wave of her magic wand? If so, you probably know that the wish you so desire is beyond your control to fulfill, and it may not be possible at all (for example, curing your sick mother of her terminal disease). Wish-fulfillment dreams may not always come true, but they have a psychological purpose.

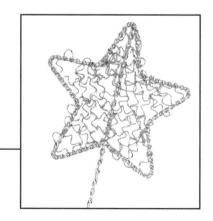

CREATURES & BEINGS

SPIRITUALITY, MAGIC & MYTH

Related themes:
Parents and step-parents
Grandmothers and grandfathers
Wisdom and experience

WITCHES & WIZARDS

The witch and wizard are both archetypal figures representing an aspect of the older woman/mother and man/father, respectively. A dream witch may thus represent an older female in your life—perhaps an authoritarian teacher or relative who you feel wields some terrible power over you. Likewise, a wizard, or wise man, in your dream may have been a manifestation of a kindly male figure, perhaps your grandfather, whose behavior in your dream may have been a message or piece of advice for you from a trusted, experienced source. Each of these archetypes have both a positive (benign) side and a negative (destructive) one.

DEATHLY HALLOWS

In your dream, did you find yourself dressed as a witch, or else taking on some traits that are traditionally associated with witches? If so, ask yourself whether you were the wise woman or a cruel witch. The answer will give you a clue as to the meaning of your dream, which probably related to your behavior in relation to someone younger than yourself, over whom you have influence.

SPIRITUALITY, MAGIC & MYTH

RELIGION

Related themes:
Awesome power
Ultimate authority
Discipline and sanctions

SUPREME BEING

One person's understanding of a "supreme being" may differ widely from the next, whether it be the mighty God of a formal religion, a creator of the universe, or a kind of life-force. Benign or vengeful, it is most often characterized as something overwhelmingly powerful that is able to intervene in our affairs. If you dream of the supreme being at a time when you feel that you are out of control, your unconscious mind may be seeking guidance from the highest spiritual level. Alternatively, there may have been a specific dream message that could help you solve a particular problem, or shame you into improving your recent behavior.

HEAVENLY ENCOUNTER
If you dreamed that the clouds parted and rays of sun appeared, did you feel that you were in the presence of your higher power and were being given a message that could relate to your waking circumstances? These dreams may occur if you believe that divine help can sustain you through a difficult time in your life, or else could warn you away from pursuing inappropriate behavior.

RELIGION

Related themes:
Archetypes
Overwhelming emotions
Special powers and abilities

GODS & GODDESSES

Gods and goddesses of many cultures, through time and around the world, share some of their characteristics with counterparts in the beliefs of other cultures. The moon, for example, is an attribute of many goddesses. Deities are similar because they are archetypal figures, embodiments of universal human emotions and behavioral patterns—of love or death, perhaps. The dreaming mind thus sees what these divine archetypes represent even if the dreamer knows little or nothing of the god or goddess that featured in the dream scene. So, if your dream featured a god or goddess, try to relate the figure to the archetypes in Chapter 1.

MOTHER GODDESS

In your dream, did you gaze upon a sculpted goddess figure and feel that she was communicating a supportive message to you, even though you did not actually recognize the identity of the goddess? Your dream may have been a message from your unconscious to boost your morale, sustaining you like a protective mother in your time of need.

SPIRITUALITY, MAGIC & MYTH

RELIGION

Related themes:
Happiness
Peace
Contentment

HEAVEN OR NIRVANA

Most dreams of being in heaven, nirvana, or a similar spiritual realm refer either to your current state of mind—if you are feeling depressed and hopeless, perhaps, or else blissfully happy—or to your outlook on your future. So, if your dreaming heaven was the polar opposite of your current situation, your dream may have been a safety valve providing temporary relief from your current trying circumstances. Alternatively, you may be embarking on what appears to be a stable and happy phase of your life, unblemished by troubles, and your dreaming mind was playing out this happy state of affairs in another form.

REALM OF LOVE

If you dreamed that you were in heaven, engaged in an activity related to nurturing and caring for others (like cooking or tending a vegetable garden, or shopping for food), have you recently become involved with a new partner after a long period of single life, or else have you just become a parent? Your dream may simply have reflected your happiness at the new role you see yourself playing in life.

RELIGION

SPIRITUALITY, MAGIC & MYTH

Related themes:
Guilt
Suffering
Remorse

HELL OR LIMBO

Like dreams of being in heaven, your dreams of hell are a reflection of your current life or of your feelings about your future. So, if you are religious and dreamed that you were burning in hell or awaiting judgment in limbo, the dream does not mean that you will be going there after your death. It is likely that your dream hell was a consequence of your waking guilt about something that you've done, or have been planning to do, despite knowing that it does not meet your moral standards. Examine your conscience to find what your unconscious was trying to tell you; the details of your dream will provide clues as to its significance.

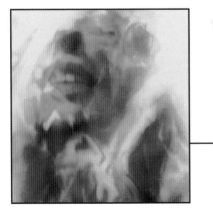

BURNING UP

If, in your dream, you were burning in the flames of a searing fire, try to identify whether you had an overriding emotion. If it was pure and simple fear, you may have been reacting to the news of a local fire disaster. Only if your dreaming emotions were dominated by feelings of guilt or remorse, and if you believe in a hell-like afterlife, was this likely to have been a dream of being in hell.

SPIRITUALITY, MAGIC & MYTH

RELIGION

Related themes:
Sanctuary
Peace
Conscience

PLACES OF WORSHIP

If you regularly attend a synagogue, church, mosque, or temple, your place of worship may feature in your dreams, perhaps giving you a feeling of comfort or support, or else pricking your conscience if you have something to confess or make amends for. But if you don't usually go to a religious building, your dream is still likely to have a spiritual interpretation. You may have entered a sanctuary in your dream as a way of escaping a pursuer. If you did so, and found a feeling of peace within its walls, the dream pursuer may represent a person you have wronged in waking life, or someone who wants something from you.

PLACE OF PEACE

Did you come upon a beautiful, serene temple in your dream and seek solace by going inside? This dream is likely to reflect your anxious or pressurized frame of mind at the moment. Are you troubled by others' demands and unsure of how to cope? If so, the dream suggests that you should make time to retreat into yourself and either think through your situation or refresh yourself with rest.

RELIGION

SPIRITUALITY, MAGIC & MYTH

Related themes:
Conscience
Guidance
Leadership

SPIRITUAL AUTHORITIES

Ministers, monks, gurus, imams, vicars, rabbis, cardinals, and priests all represent spiritual authority, and their appearance in our dreams usually carries a particular message. Were you uneasy because the leader reminded you of a neglected moral responsibility toward someone (maybe even yourself)? Have you done something recently that you now feel guilty about? Or are you unconsciously yearning for some spiritual guidance in an area of your life? Although these are profoundly difficult questions to ask yourself, only you can provide the key to the meaning of such dreams, because they are profoundly personal.

MORAL MONK

When you dream of encountering a spiritual authority figure or asking one for help with a decision, your unconscious may have been representing your own conscience in the form of the dream monk or minister. So if you were given a pearl of wisdom in answer to your dilemma, it is likely that this advice came from somewhere within yourself.

SPIRITUALITY, MAGIC & MYTH

RELIGION

Related themes:
Peace
Wish fulfillment
Guidance

PRAYING AND MEDITATING

When we dream of prayer and meditation, the most likely explanation for this is the build-up of pressure in waking life either to find some mental space and time to focus on ourselves, or to seek an answer to a particular problem or dilemma. Praying is most likely to involve the quest for an outcome, whether it be granting a deep-seated wish or giving aid in a task or lifestyle choice that we are finding especially hard, such as quitting a harmful habit. On the other hand, dream meditation points to the need for some peace amid the hectic pace of daily life, or else for enlightenment and a greater understanding of people around us.

A LITTLE PRAYER

In your dream, did you see yourself praying intently, yet you don't pray in waking life? If so, are you facing an impossible problem that you don't know how to deal with? The fact that you engaged in prayer in your dream is an indication that you are hopeful of a solution to your problem, even if you don't know how to go about finding it. Was there a dream clue to the answers?

FESTIVALS & RITES

SPIRITUALITY, MAGIC & MYTH

Related themes:
Comfort
Conforming
Rebellion

RELIGIOUS RITES & CEREMONIES

If you were a member of a dream congregation or participated in, or witnessed, a religious rite, your dream reaction is paramount. Depending on your current situation, the feeling of being comforted, or uplifted, or blessed could either denote your joy at being in harmony with a prevailing moral code or, alternatively, a deep-rooted desire to fall in line with the attitudes and beliefs of the rest of the flock. If your reaction was one of rejection or rebellion, however, your unconscious mind may be urging you to assert your individuality, which is perhaps being stifled by the strictures of a collective belief system.

COMMUNAL CEREMONY

Did you dream that you were witnessing, or else participating in, a religious ceremony whose meaning was not clear to you? If you were processing in a line with others, wearing long robes and chanting scriptural verses, could it be that you are involved in a situation in the real world with rigid codes of behavior that you feel restricted by?

SPIRITUALITY,
MAGIC & MYTH

Related themes:
Protection
Fantasy
Special powers

FESTIVALS & RITES

MAGICAL RITUALS

When you dream of magic, the most important reference may be to the identity of the magician, if there was one. If you were casting spells yourself, do you secretly wish that you had special powers to solve a problem or fulfill your wishes when your actual talents prove insufficiently potent? If, on the other hand, you dreamed that your friend had developed magical powers, is he or she someone who might bewitch you, or coerce you subtly to do what he or she wants in the waking world? Or perhaps you dreamed of a magic circle or wand: the circle signifies protection (*see also* page 350), while wands may have phallic connotations.

BOLT FROM THE BLUE

In your dream, did you suddenly see a bolt of lightning or flash of colored light crossing your line of vision? This may have signified a flash of inspiration or an epiphany, and if you can remember the context in which you dreamed of it, it may yield a clue to something you've been trying to work out. But if you were filled with a sense of foreboding, it may have been a sign of someone's ill intent.

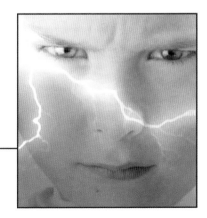

FESTIVALS & RITES

SPIRITUALITY, MAGIC & MYTH

Related themes:
Celebration
Family
The seasons

HOLIDAYS AND SEASONAL FESTIVALS

Festivals and annual holidays communicate different messages in dreams, depending on the beliefs of the individual dreamer and the emotions experienced during the dream. If you are a Christian, for example, your dream of a joyful Christmas may reflect your desire to be reborn in your faith; or if you hold pagan beliefs, a dream of spring celebrations could indicate your need to reconnect with the earth in some way. If you do not hold strong religious beliefs, or if you dreamed of a secular holiday like Thanksgiving, the meaning is more likely to have been connected to your family relationships, past or present.

FEAST OR FAMINE?

Did your dream of sitting down to your Thanksgiving dinner fill you with dread? If so, this is likely to reflect tensions in your family. Does your sister suffer from an eating disorder, for example, and do you dread making food the focus of your day? Or do you strongly dislike your divorced parent's new partner? Dreams like these simply mirror your waking anxieties about your loved ones.

SPIRITUAL & MYTHICAL

SPIRITUALITY,
MAGIC & MYTH

SPECIAL POWERS

Related themes:
Powerlessness
Wish fulfillment
The archetypal hero or amazon

SUPERNATURAL STRENGTH

Did you awake from a dream in which a superhuman hero rescued someone from peril? If so, were you the hero or the person who was rescued? If you were rescued by a kind of superhero figure, your unconscious may have indulged you by conjuring up a fantasy solution to an intractable real-life problem, in order to bring you some temporary solace or relief. If, however, you suddenly found incredible strength and managed to save someone else from danger, try to remember or work out the identity of the person you rescued. Your unconscious may be hinting that he or she needs your help or is at risk in real life.

BULGING BICEPS
If you are a man, and you dreamed that you had developed powerful muscles, were you bullied during your schooldays, and has someone recently triggered the humiliating memories you've repressed about those experiences? If you have been made to feel powerless at work or by the arrival of a dominating figure on your social scene, this dream may have been encouraging you to stand tall.

SPECIAL POWERS

Related themes:
Emotional closeness
Intuition
Separations

TELEPATHY

Telepathic communication is said to occur between people who are emotionally close at times of need or crisis. So, for example, a twin may suddenly be aware of the other's pain, accident or heartache despite the fact that no physical or virtual communication has taken place. Some people claim to have experienced telepathic dreams of this sort, although there is no scientific explanation for telepathic dreaming. But did you dream that you had developed power of telepathy? If so, and your brother or husband recently set off for active military service in another country, your ability to make dream telepathic contact was a wish fulfillment.

PSYCHIC POWERS
Dreams that involve conversing with a lost loved one through psychic powers, or through a medium with these powers, are often experienced by people who have been recently bereaved. The feeling of being reunited with him or her by experiencing this connection can be so powerful that the dreamer may awake convinced that the reunion was real, and comforted by the communication.

SPECIAL
POWERS

Related themes:
Peace
Happiness
Wish fulfillment

HEALING

Was your dream of healing or being healed related to physical or spiritual well-being? If you have been desperately worried about your partner's ill health in real life, and you dreamed of having supernatural powers to cure him or her, your dream was a wish fulfillment. But did you dream that you were approached by a healer who told you that you needed psychic healing, and did he or she then lay hands on you and induce a powerful sense of well-being? If so, try to be honest with yourself about what your unconscious has detected about your current emotional state. Have you been driving yourself too hard, or burying your misery?

HEALING HANDS

If you dreamed that you could heal people, and your "patients" were not known to you, could you be harboring desires to change the course of your career and train to work in a caring profession instead of continuing with your clerical job? Or have you been watching distressing news items about a war zone or a natural disaster? If this is the case, your dream mirrors your waking concerns.

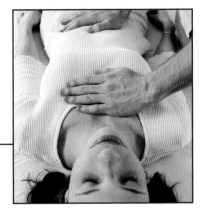

RECORDING YOUR DREAMS

Learning to decode your dreams is a fascinating and rewarding pursuit, but your skills will be wasted if you are unable to remember in sufficient detail what you dreamed of. It's crucial that you record your dreams immediately upon waking, because your memory of them fades quickly.

Whether you document only one dream a week or write up the dream, or dreams, that you have every night, keeping a dream diary will not only preserve the dreams that your unique, unconscious mind has generated, but will enable you to keep track of your experiences in dreamland and thus also of your state of mind. Consulting your dream diary will furthermore enable you to discern the patterns that underlie your dreams, to recognize your emotional reaction to certain situations, and then take conscious steps either to improve your waking circumstances or to face them more positively. If you work regular office hours in the waking world, and an examination of your dream diary reveals that you repeatedly have nightmares in the small hours of Monday morning, for instance, your journal may at last have enabled your conscious self to grasp what you have unconsciously known for some time, that is, that you find your working hours "a nightmare." Based on the advice from your unconscious, you may then either decide to leave your job or find a way of actively controlling, rather than passively suffering, its challenges.

YOUR DREAM DIARY

How you record your dreams initially is partly a matter of your own circumstances and preferences: you can keep a notebook or a file of blank, photocopied or printed journal pages by your bedside so that you can make notes or write up your nighttime adventures when you wake up, or you can use recording equipment. If you choose the latter method, you will then have to transcribe your spoken words into a written dream diary in order to study them (which you may also need to do if you scribble brief notes).

Once you have recorded your dream on paper, you may find that you are left with a mass of notes and doodles that is difficult to decipher. If so, consider copying your dreamwork into a second journal to keep as a neater, more permanent, ongoing record to which you will find it easier to refer when trying to identify recurring patterns. This "official" dream journal could take the form of a large, hardback notebook or word-processed computer files, and the advantage of using a computer is that you can run a search for key words or dates when trying to link one dream with another. If you decide to keep both a rough and an "official" dream diary in tandem, don't throw your original notes away, however, because there may be occasions when you want to compare the two.

Whatever form your dream diary takes, it's best to allocate two pages to each dream, one containing a list of headings and the other a blank page—ideally, the notebook's facing page if you keep your diary in book form—on which to write your interpretation of your dream.

REMEMBERING YOUR DREAMS

You have, no doubt, already found that your dreams tend to disappear from your memory almost as soon as you get up. When your conscious mind takes control of your body again, it is so busy focusing on the day ahead that it tunes out, and then swiftly erases, your unconscious recollection of the events that occurred in dreamland the previous night. Although tantalizing echoes of your dream may still linger in your mind, or be triggered during the day, echoes do not provide sufficient material with which to work when exploring your dreams in depth, which is why it's important to try to remain in the frame of mind that prompted your dreams in the first place when you are recording them.

Although simply becoming interested in your dreams will stimulate your powers of recollection, there are two useful methods that you could use in conjunction with each other to help you to remember your dreams long enough to log them accurately. First, you could try programming your unconscious mind to recall your dreams using autosuggestion, maybe by saying to yourself, "I will remember my dream when I wake up" just before dropping off to sleep. Second, as soon as you are aware of having become conscious during the night or early morning, lie still and let your mind drift until you are immersed in the memory of your dream. Now is the point at which you should slowly, but immediately, reach for your flashlight, pen, and dream diary, or else your recording device, and start recording your dream.

WRITING UP YOUR DREAMS

As soon as you are ready to record the details, let the words flow, whether they escape from your unconscious mind in a torrent or in only a few key words or phrases that describe the theme of the dream or your dreaming mood. Work as quickly as you can, and try not to let any conscious thoughts intrude as you place your dream on record, because even pausing to try to think of an apt word can frequently cause the memory of your dream to fade frustratingly rapidly. And if you find it easier to sketch, rather than verbally describe, an aspect of your dream, then do so. If possible, also write down the time at which you awoke, because if you end up document-ing a series of dreams that night, the order in which they occurred may be significant. Once you have made these notes, you can decipher its meaning later in the day.

When you return to your dreamwork (preferably on the same day), write up your dream as fully as you can from your original notes—ideally preserving its immediacy by using the present tense—also re-creating any drawings that you may have made. There are certain additional details that you should always log, notably the *day and date* on which the dream occurred, along with the *time* when it ended, if you wrote it down. The combination of these details with your description of your dream will enable you to compare your dream diary with a calendar to see if you can discern whether any specific events in the real world prompted your dream, or gave rise to a dreaming pattern, and, if you think that they did, to learn to understand your emotional response to these trigger situations. For this reason, too, it is important to record the *atmosphere* that pervaded your dream (threatening, wet, or sunny, for example), along with your dreaming self's *mood* (such as scared or relaxed). You should also *number* your dreams in the order in which you had them.

Having completed the bare bones of a page in your dream diary, writing down significant elements of your dream under separate headings may both help you to decode your dream and highlight potentially recurring themes or symbols for future reference. It is useful to write down the *time* in which the dream was set (day or night, the season, the past, present, or future, for instance); any *colors* that caught your dreaming attention; whether *movement* was an important aspect of your dream (were you running, climbing, flying, falling, or undertaking a journey, for example?); the *setting*; any *people, animals, buildings, objects, signs,* or *symbols* (road signs, vehicles, or shapes, for instance) that featured in your dream; and any *words* you may remember.

Further information that it is always helpful to record is *what happened yesterday, how you were feeling yesterday*, and *a possible trigger for the dream* because these details may help you to pinpoint your unconscious response to real-life events. You may also find that giving your dream a *title* or theme and deciding on its *type* proves useful when looking for patterns in your dreams. Remember, however, that the format of this dream diary is only a guide, and you may prefer to devise your own diary format and headings.

ANALYZING YOUR DREAMS

By filling in a page of your dream diary in this way, you have now created both a record of your dream and one of the best starting points for its analysis. Using a new page, jot down your thoughts about the meaning of your dream, using this book and other tools, like dictionaries and encyclopedias, free and direct association, or describing your dream to, and maybe discussing it with, someone else. Above all, however, remember to try to think as intuitively as possible because this way you'll be tapping into your unconscious (after all, the source of your dream). And when you think that you have found a likely explanation for anything that seemed significant in your dream, try to explain why you have reached your conclusion because this will help you to understand the symbolic language that is personal to you (if you dreamed of a cat, for example, and you are feline-phobic, write down your dislike of these creatures).

When you have finished, sit back and consider the message that you believe your unconscious was sending you before entering it at the bottom of the page. Does it make perfect sense in the context of your waking world? Or has it made you think about changing an aspect of your life? Don't be discouraged if the meaning of your dream eludes you, however. Not only will you find that the interpretation process becomes easier with practice, but your dream diary may later reveal that your baffling dream is one of a sequence of similar dreams that has either yet to unfold or whose meaning you have not yet grasped.

Day and Date _____ Time _____ Number _____

Dream Title _____

Type of Dream _____

Atmosphere _____

My Dreaming Mood _____

_____

Narrative of Events _____

_____

_____

Time _____

Colors _____

Movement _____

Setting _____

_____

People _____

_____

Animals _____

Buildings _____

Objects _____

Other Significant Signs or Symbols _____

Words or Puns _____

What Happened Yesterday _____

_____

How I was Feeling Yesterday _____

_____

A Possible Trigger for the Dream _____

_____

Possible Link with Dream Number(s) _____